ESSENTIAL MATHEMATICS
FOR
ECONOMICS
A Student's Guide to
Key Mathematical Techniques

ESSENTIAL MATHEMATICS FOR ECONOMICS

A Student's Guide to Key Mathematical Techniques

VASILEIOS ZIKOS

Chulalongkorn University, Thailand

World Scientific

NEW JERSEY • LONDON • SINGAPORE • BEIJING • SHANGHAI • HONG KONG • TAIPEI • CHENNAI • TOKYO

Published by

World Scientific Publishing Co. Pte. Ltd.
5 Toh Tuck Link, Singapore 596224
USA office: 27 Warren Street, Suite 401-402, Hackensack, NJ 07601
UK office: 57 Shelton Street, Covent Garden, London WC2H 9HE

Library of Congress Control Number: 2025039108

British Library Cataloguing-in-Publication Data
A catalogue record for this book is available from the British Library.

ESSENTIAL MATHEMATICS FOR ECONOMICS
A Student's Guide to Key Mathematical Techniques

ISBN 978-981-98-1410-7 (hardcover)
ISBN 978-981-98-1483-1 (paperback)
ISBN 978-981-98-1411-4 (ebook for institutions)
ISBN 978-981-98-1412-1 (ebook for individuals)

For any available supplementary material, please visit
https://www.worldscientific.com/worldscibooks/10.1142/14339#t=suppl

Desk Editors: Eshak Nabi Akbar Ali/Yulin Jiang

Typeset by Stallion Press
Email: enquiries@stallionpress.com

ABOUT THE AUTHOR

Vasileios Zikos is Professor of Economics at Chulalongkorn University and Chief Editor of the *Southeast Asian Journal of Economics.* He holds a Postgraduate Certificate in Academic Practice, awarded with Distinction by the University of Surrey and the Higher Education Academy. Over the past two decades, he has taught undergraduate and graduate courses in microeconomics and mathematics. His research lies in applied microeconomics, with a particular focus on the interactions among health, the environment, and subjective well-being, and their implications for economic outcomes and public policy.

INTRODUCTION

Purpose and Style

Every author has in mind potential readers of his or her work who could benefit after having read it. Mine is advanced undergraduate and first-year graduate students in economics. I hope to enrich how these students use mathematics when they formulate economic problems, especially in the area of microeconomics. Many existing textbooks offer an advanced treatment of the topic, while others are elementary and may lack rigor. The problem with both approaches is that they do not allow students to develop their mathematical skills systematically or familiarize themselves with the art of formal reasoning.

To study how consumers, firms, and societies make decisions, economists build formal models. A formal model is a simplified way to analyze economic phenomena occurring in the real world. However, reality is quite complex, and for this reason, economic models rely on simplifying assumptions. A key element in building a good model is understanding the most important aspects of the phenomenon being studied. Thinking within such a structured framework can be challenging and involves learning a new language: the language of mathematics.

With this in mind, I have chosen topics that are essential for understanding and applying mathematics, particularly in microeconomics. I provide an example with its solution immediately following each new concept presented. The goal is to introduce mathematical concepts and tools gradually while developing a language for thinking about economic problems. This book is self-contained, and all required methods of analysis are explained within the text. Additional exercises at the end of each chapter offer further practice on key concepts.

An important objective in microeconomics is to understand how consumers, firms, and societies make decisions regarding the allocation of scarce resources. Consumers are assumed to maximize their utility or satisfaction derived from consuming goods, subject to a budget constraint. Likewise, firms strive to maximize their profits while considering resource constraints. Governments aim to maximize the welfare of their citizens by implementing policies that influence resource allocation and market outcomes.

Much of the discussion in this book focuses on developing tools for solving such problems. However, it is important to recognize that there are alternative motivations for both consumer and firm behavior that can also be modelled mathematically. For instance, consumers may engage in satisficing — aiming for satisfactory outcomes rather than optimal ones — while firms might prioritize market share maximization over profit maximization. The mathematical techniques developed in this book are applicable not only to traditional models focused on utility and profit maximization but also to these alternative frameworks.

My aim for this book is to improve students' ability to formulate economic problems and provide essential mathematical tools for analysis across various contexts. This book presents my current understanding of mathematics, shaped by several years of teaching this subject. Over those years, I have been fortunate to interact with many excellent students, and this book has naturally been informed by those discussions. I have attempted to reorganize and rewrite several parts of the text in light of students' questions, aiming to better highlight key concepts and provide additional clarity when possible. In this way, my hope is that students will feel more guided in their study of mathematics and its economic applications.

I am also grateful to the following individuals (listed in alphabetical order) for their thoughtful suggestions and insights: Rifaan Ahmed, Marios Choudetsanakis, Tian Guowei, Dusanee Kesavayuth, Doori Kim, Kaung Myat Ko, Vijit Kunapongkul, Joanna Poyago-Theotoky, James Stankovich, and Dai Binh Tran. Their feedback has contributed meaningfully to the development of this text. Finally, I would like to thank Yulin Jiang at World Scientific for his patience, professionalism, and careful attention during the revision and production of the manuscript.

Structure of the Book

The book is divided into nine chapters. Chapter 1 begins by elaborating on the distinction between necessary and sufficient conditions used to describe how two statements are related. The chapter then presents the basic elements of matrix algebra, including matrix operations, transposes, inverses, minors, cofactors, and determinants. These concepts are introduced through examples designed to help students understand how to apply them directly. The main focus of the chapter is on elements of matrix algebra that will be useful in subsequent parts of the book, especially when solving optimization problems.

Chapter 2 is concerned with the study of differential calculus. A primary objective is to find the derivative of a function, a process known as differentiation. One important application of derivatives is in identifying the extreme values of a function. The chapter also introduces the concept of the partial derivative, which describes how a function changes with respect to one variable while holding all other variables constant. I then explore the concept of the total derivative, which becomes relevant when there is a functional relationship among the independent variables of a function. In such cases, the total derivative accounts for all possible channels — both direct and indirect — through which changes in one variable affect the dependent variable. This chapter also presents an implicit function theorem, which provides conditions under which an implicit function can be derived from a given equation. The theorem is applied to compute partial derivatives, including the slope of an indifference curve and the slope of an isoquant.

Chapter 3 aims to bring the reader closer to the study of optimization problems by examining the shape of functions with one or more optimal points. An objective is to first introduce and discuss the concept of a convex set, which is essential as concave or convex functions typically need their domains to be a convex set. The chapter then describes conditions under which a function is concave or convex. For a function of one variable, the second derivative provides a straightforward condition for concavity and convexity, while for functions of more than one variable, the Hessian matrix is employed. Furthermore, I provide a generalization of concavity (convexity) by describing conditions under which a function is quasi-concave (quasi-convex); all concave functions are quasi-concave, but not all quasi-concave functions are necessarily concave.

The focus of Chapters 4–6 is on optimization problems. Chapter 4 discusses unconstrained optimization problems. Chapters 5 and 6 develop cases where an objective function is optimized subject to at least one equality or inequality constraint. These chapters present necessary and sufficient conditions for solving such problems. For an unconstrained optimization problem, the first-order conditions correspond to the first-order partial derivatives of the objective function with respect to each choice variable, and these partial derivatives are set to zero. These first-order conditions are necessary and provide candidate points for a local optimum. Second-order conditions are then invoked to determine the exact type of each candidate point based on the signs of the principal minors of the Hessian matrix.

Chapter 5 deals with optimization problems that have equality constraints, meaning that these constraints are always binding: they are satisfied with equality. As we will see, the Lagrange multiplier method is employed to solve such problems. The first-order conditions are derived by taking the partial derivatives of the Lagrangian function with respect to each choice variable and each Lagrange multiplier, and setting them equal to zero. These conditions yield candidate points for a local optimum, in much the same way as in unconstrained optimization. Second-order conditions, based on the signs of the principal minors of the bordered Hessian matrix, can be used to determine the exact type of each candidate point.

Chapter 6 extends methods for solving constrained optimization problems to include inequality constraints. For example, a consumer may wish to spend some, but not all, of her budget, or a firm may use only part of its available resources. In both cases, the constraint functions would not be satisfied as equalities. With equality constraints, the first-order conditions are derived by taking the first-order partial derivatives of the Lagrangian function with respect to each choice variable and the Lagrange multiplier, and then setting them to zero. Similar types of conditions apply with inequality constraints and are known as Kuhn–Tucker conditions. However, while the first-order conditions in optimization problems with equality constraints are necessary for a solution, the Kuhn–Tucker conditions must satisfy certain requirements to qualify as necessary. Furthermore, this chapter discusses circumstances under which the Kuhn–Tucker conditions are not only necessary but also sufficient.

In Chapters 7 and 8, we shift the focus from static analysis to dynamic analysis. In the static models from Chapters 5 and 6, the goal was to maximize or minimize an objective function subject to one or more constraints. The first-order conditions characterized optimal solutions and served as equilibrium conditions. In dynamic analysis, by contrast, the goal is to study the time paths of specific variables and determine whether they converge to specific values if sufficient time is allowed. In this context, we begin the analysis without assuming that an equilibrium exists a priori. Instead, starting with a pattern of change that describes the behavior of a variable, we examine the adjustment process to a specific value and determine whether an equilibrium exists. Thus, we seek to identify the complete trajectory of a variable, such as investment or price. The solution to this problem is a function that traces the path of the variable of interest over time.

Starting with a pattern of change and tracing a time path requires uncovering the primitive function from a derived function. For simple cases, this can be done using integral calculus, which is generally the reverse process of the differentiation method studied in Chapter 2. For more complicated cases, we will turn to the techniques of differential equations. We will first study integration techniques in Chapter 7 and then proceed to consider simple differential equations in Chapter 8.

The final chapter of this book explores applications of the mathematical techniques studied in the previous chapters, drawing examples primarily from two of my own research articles. The first example comes from the area of industrial organization, which employs concepts from game theory to study strategic interactions between agents. Agents can be thought of as players in a game involving one or more stages of strategic interaction. As we will see, the study of such interactions relies on two main techniques: differentiation and optimization.

The second example comes from another area of research: the economics of well-being. I examine the link between subjective well-being and physical health, and discuss how this link can be explained by "third" variables, known as mediators. The main hypothesis posits that people's well-being influences their physical health not only directly but also indirectly. Total derivatives, as studied in Chapter 2, account for all possible channels — both direct and indirect — through which the effect of an independent variable is transmitted to the dependent variable. This observation will be useful for setting up an empirical test of the hypothesis that the effects of subjective well-being on physical health are mediated by different types of health investments. While the first example is theoretical in nature, the second is empirical. The choice of both examples is deliberate and aims to demonstrate that mathematics has immediate applications in many areas of economics.

CONTENTS

About the Author v

Introduction vii

Purpose and Style vii
Structure of the Book ix

CHAPTER 1: LINEAR ALGEBRA 1

Learning Objectives 1
1.1 Necessary and Sufficient Conditions 2
1.1.1 Necessary conditions 2
1.1.2 Sufficient conditions 2
1.1.3 Necessary and sufficient conditions 3
1.2 Matrix Algebra 3
1.2.1 Basics of matrix algebra 3
1.2.2 Matrix operations 4
1.2.2.1 Matrix addition 4
1.2.2.2 Scalar multiplication 4
1.2.2.3 Matrix multiplication 5
1.2.3 Laws of matrix operations 6
1.2.3.1 Laws of matrix addition 6
1.2.3.2 Laws of matrix multiplication 7
1.2.4 Special types of matrices 7
1.2.4.1 Identity matrix 7
1.2.4.2 Null matrix 8
1.2.5 Transpose of a matrix 9
1.2.6 Inverse matrix 10
1.2.7 Determinants 12
1.2.7.1 Minors 12
1.2.7.2 Cofactors 13
1.2.7.3 Adjoint (adjugate) of a matrix 14
1.2.7.4 Evaluating a second-order determinant 16
1.2.7.5 Evaluating a higher-order determinant 16

1.3 Further Exercises and Applications 18
Further Reading 23

CHAPTER 2: DIFFERENTIAL CALCULUS **25**

Learning Objectives 25
2.1 The Concept of Derivative 26
2.1.1 Rules of derivatives for functions with a single variable . . 27
2.2 Differentiation of Functions with Multiple Variables 28
2.2.1 Partial differentiation 28
2.2.2 Total differentials and total derivatives 30
2.2.2.1 Total differentials 30
2.2.2.2 Rules of differentials 31
2.2.2.3 Total derivatives 31
2.2.2.4 Chain rule for composite functions 33
2.3 An Implicit Function Theorem 34
2.4 Further Exercises and Applications 36
Further Reading 38

CHAPTER 3: CONCAVITY AND CONVEXITY OF FUNCTIONS **39**

Learning Objectives 39
3.1 Convex Sets 40
3.2 Concavity and Convexity 41
3.2.1 Checking concavity and convexity 42
3.2.2 Functions of n variables 45
3.2.3 Conditions using the Hessian matrix 47
3.2.4 Theorems on concavity and convexity 49
3.3 Quasi-Concavity and Quasi-Convexity 49
3.3.1 Theorems on quasi-concavity and quasi-convexity 51
3.3.2 Conditions for quasi-concavity and quasi-convexity 52
3.4 Further Exercises and Applications 54
Further Reading 56

CHAPTER 4: UNCONSTRAINED OPTIMIZATION **57**

Learning Objectives 57
4.1 Functions of More Than One Variable 58
4.2 Functions of One Variable 63
4.3 An Envelope Theorem 66
4.4 Further Exercises and Applications 68
Further Reading 71

CHAPTER 5: OPTIMIZATION WITH EQUALITY CONSTRAINTS **73**

Learning Objectives . . . 73
5.1 Constrained Extreme Points and the Lagrange Multiplier . . . 74
5.2 Second-Order Conditions and the Bordered Hessian Matrix . . . 76
5.3 Multiple Constraints . . . 79
5.4 Interpreting the Lagrange Multiplier . . . 81
5.5 Further Exercises and Applications . . . 84
Further Reading . . . 87

CHAPTER 6: OPTIMIZATION WITH INEQUALITY CONSTRAINTS **89**

Learning Objectives . . . 89
6.1 The Kuhn–Tucker Conditions . . . 90
6.2 Solving the Optimization Problem . . . 95
6.3 Necessity of the Kuhn–Tucker Conditions . . . 98
6.4 Sufficiency of the Kuhn–Tucker Conditions . . . 100
6.5 Further Exercises and Applications . . . 102
Further Reading . . . 105

CHAPTER 7: INTEGRAL CALCULUS **107**

Learning Objectives . . . 107
7.1 The Concept of Integration . . . 108
7.2 Basic Rules of Integration . . . 110
7.2.1 Rule I: The power rule . . . 110
7.2.2 Rule II: The logarithmic rule . . . 111
7.2.3 Rule III: The exponential rule . . . 112
7.2.4 Rule IV: The sum-difference rule . . . 112
7.2.5 Rule V: The multiplication by a constant rule . . . 113
7.3 Rules Involving Substitution . . . 113
7.3.1 Rule VI: The substitution rule . . . 113
7.3.2 Rule VII: Integration by parts . . . 115
7.4 Definite Integrals: The Area under a Curve . . . 117
7.5 Properties of Definite Integrals . . . 120
7.5.1 Property I: Interchanging the limits of integration . . . 120
7.5.2 Property II: Identical limits of integration . . . 120
7.5.3 Property III: Sum of definite integrals . . . 121
7.6 Improper Integrals . . . 122
7.6.1 Infinite limit of integration . . . 122
7.6.2 Infinite integrand . . . 123
7.7 Further Exercises and Applications . . . 124
Further Reading . . . 131

CHAPTER 8: ECONOMIC DYNAMICS AND FIRST-ORDER LINEAR DIFFERENTIAL EQUATIONS **133**

Learning Objectives . . . 133
8.1 The Concept of First-Order Linear Differential Equations . . . 134
8.2 Constant Coefficient and Constant Term . . . 134
8.2.1 The homogeneous case . . . 134
8.2.2 The non-homogeneous case . . . 136
8.2.3 Verification of the solution . . . 139
8.3 Dynamics of Market Price . . . 140
8.4 Variable Coefficient and Variable Term . . . 143
8.4.1 The homogeneous case . . . 144
8.4.2 The non-homogeneous case . . . 146
8.4.3 Exact differential equations . . . 148
8.4.4 Integrating factor . . . 151
8.4.5 Applying the four-step solution procedure . . . 153
8.5 Further Exercises and Applications . . . 156
Further Reading . . . 159

CHAPTER 9: RESEARCH APPLICATIONS **161**

Learning Objectives . . . 161
9.1 Example: R&D Subsidies, Spillovers, and Privatization . . . 162
9.1.1 The model . . . 163
9.1.1.1 Preliminaries . . . 163
9.1.1.2 Sequencing of moves . . . 164
9.1.1.3 R&D investments and production costs . . . 164
9.1.1.4 Profit functions and social welfare . . . 166
9.1.2 A private duopoly market . . . 166
9.1.2.1 Output decisions . . . 166
9.1.2.2 R&D investment decisions . . . 167
9.1.2.3 R&D subsidy decision . . . 168
9.1.3 A mixed duopoly market . . . 169
9.1.3.1 Output decisions . . . 169
9.1.3.2 R&D investment decisions . . . 170
9.1.3.3 R&D subsidy decision . . . 171
9.1.4 Main results . . . 173
9.2 Example: Subjective Well-Being and Physical Health . . . 175
9.2.1 Data and description of the main variables . . . 178
9.2.2 Empirical model . . . 179
9.2.3 Results . . . 183
9.2.4 Discussion . . . 190
Further Reading . . . 192

Index 197

CHAPTER 1

LINEAR ALGEBRA

Learning Objectives

After completing this chapter, students will be able to:

- Understand necessary and sufficient conditions.
- Perform matrix operations.
- Derive the transpose of a matrix.
- Derive the inverse of a matrix.
- Calculate cofactors and determinants.

This chapter focuses on the study of necessary and sufficient conditions, as well as the basic concepts of matrix algebra.[1] It begins by explaining the distinction between necessary and sufficient conditions, and how they describe the relationship between two statements. The chapter then introduces the basic elements of matrix algebra, emphasizing concepts that will be useful later in the book, especially for solving optimization problems.

[1] This chapter follows the orientation of Bryant (2023, Chapter 1), which introduces foundational concepts in the microeconomics of choice, such as necessary and sufficient conditions and set theory. These concepts provide essential context for the mathematical tools discussed here, including matrices and their applications.

1.1 Necessary and Sufficient Conditions

1.1.1 *Necessary conditions*

A necessary condition serves as a prerequisite or screening device. Suppose that a statement X is true only if another statement N is true. This means that N is a necessary condition for X. We can express this relationship as

$$X \Rightarrow N.$$

Thus, we have

- X is true only if N is true
- "X only if N"
- "if X, then N" or "X implies N"

Example: Consider two statements, "a person is a mother" and "a person is female". The former implies the latter; that is, "a person is a mother" ⇒ "a person is female". A person is a mother only if she is female, meaning that being female is a necessary condition for motherhood.

1.1.2 *Sufficient conditions*

We now consider a situation where statement X is true if N is true, but X can still be true even when N is not true. In this case, N is said to be a sufficient condition for X. The truth of N suffices to establish the truth of X. This relationship can be expressed as

$$X \Leftarrow N.$$

Thus, we can write

- X is true if N is true, but X can also be true when N is not true
- "if N, then X" or "N implies X"

Example: Consider the statements "one can get to Thailand" and "one takes a plane to Thailand". The latter implies the former; that is, "one can get to Thailand" $\Leftarrow$ "one takes a plane to Thailand". One can get to Thailand if one takes a plane, though it is also possible to do so by other means of transportation. In other words, taking a plane is a sufficient condition for getting to Thailand.

1.1.3 *Necessary and sufficient conditions*

A third possibility is that the statement N is both necessary and sufficient for statement X. This relationship can be expressed as

$$X \Leftrightarrow N.$$

Accordingly, we say X if and only if (iff) N, which also implies that $X \Rightarrow N$ and $N \Rightarrow X$.

Example: Consider the statements "There are less than 30 days in the month" and "It is the month of February". We can write "There are less than 30 days in the month" $\Leftrightarrow$ "It is the month of February".

1.2 Matrix Algebra

1.2.1 *Basics of matrix algebra*

A matrix is a collection of elements organized into rows and columns, typically enclosed in brackets. More specifically, a matrix can be defined as a two-dimensional rectangular array of real numbers, complex numbers, or other mathematical symbols.

$$\boldsymbol{A} = \begin{pmatrix} a_{11} & a_{12} & \cdots & a_{1n} \\ a_{21} & a_{22} & \cdots & a_{2n} \\ \vdots & \vdots & \ddots & \vdots \\ a_{m1} & a_{m2} & \cdots & a_{mn} \end{pmatrix}_{m\times n}.$$

An alternative representation of a matrix is $\boldsymbol{A} = (a_{ij})_{m\times n}$ for $i = 1\ldots, m$ and $j = 1,\ldots, n$. If there are n columns, each containing m elements (or m rows, each containing n elements), we say that the dimension of matrix $\boldsymbol{A}$ is $m \times n$. In the special case where $m = n$, the matrix is referred to as a square matrix.

1.2.2 *Matrix operations*

First, let us define equality between two matrices. Two matrices $\boldsymbol{A} = (a_{ij})$ and $\boldsymbol{B} = (b_{ij})$ are said to be equal if and only if they have the same dimensions and identical elements in corresponding positions within the arrays.

Definition: Matrix $\boldsymbol{A}$ is equal to a matrix $\boldsymbol{B}$ if and only if $\boldsymbol{A}$ and $\boldsymbol{B}$ are of the same dimension and $a_{ij} = b_{ij}\,\forall\, i, j$, where the symbol $\forall$ means "for every" or "for all".

Next, we define three matrix operations: addition, subtraction, and multiplication between two matrices as well as multiplication of a matrix by a scalar.

1.2.2.1 *Matrix addition*

Addition (subtraction) of two matrices $\boldsymbol{A}$ and $\boldsymbol{B}$ of the same dimension $m\times n$ is the operation of adding (subtracting) their corresponding elements.

$$\text{Given } \boldsymbol{A} = (a_{ij})_{m\times n} \text{ and } \boldsymbol{B} = (b_{ij})_{m\times n}, \text{ then}$$

$$\boldsymbol{A} \pm \boldsymbol{B} = (a_{ij} \pm b_{ij})_{m\times n}.$$

1.2.2.2 *Scalar multiplication*

Multiplication of a matrix by a scalar is the operation of multiplying each element of the matrix by a real number.

$$\lambda \boldsymbol{A} = \lambda(a_{ij})_{m\times n}.$$

1.2.2.3 *Matrix multiplication*

Multiplication of two matrices can be performed if and only if the dimensions of the matrices are compatible. The compatibility condition for multiplication requires that the number of columns in matrix $\boldsymbol{A}$ equals the number of rows in matrix $\boldsymbol{B}$. In this context, we assume that matrix $\boldsymbol{A}$ is the "lead" matrix and matrix $\boldsymbol{B}$ is the "lag" matrix in the expression $\boldsymbol{A} \cdot \boldsymbol{B}$ or simply $\boldsymbol{AB}$. Thus, if $\boldsymbol{A} = (a_{ij})_{m\times r}$ and $\boldsymbol{B} = (b_{ij})_{r\times n}$, then the product is given by $\boldsymbol{AB} = \boldsymbol{C} = (c_{ij})_{m\times n}$. It is also important to distinguish between pre-multiplication and post-multiplication. In the product $\boldsymbol{AB}$, the matrix $\boldsymbol{A}$ is post-multiplied by $\boldsymbol{B}$ (or, equivalently, $\boldsymbol{B}$ is pre-multiplied by $\boldsymbol{A}$).

$$\boldsymbol{A} = \begin{pmatrix} a_{11} & a_{12} & \cdots & a_{1r} \\ a_{21} & a_{22} & \cdots & a_{2r} \\ \vdots & \vdots & \ddots & \vdots \\ a_{m1} & a_{m2} & \cdots & a_{mr} \end{pmatrix}_{m\times r} \cdot \boldsymbol{B} = \begin{pmatrix} b_{11} & b_{12} & \cdots & b_{1n} \\ b_{21} & b_{22} & \cdots & b_{2n} \\ \vdots & \vdots & \ddots & \vdots \\ b_{r1} & b_{r2} & \cdots & b_{rn} \end{pmatrix}_{r\times n}$$

$$\boldsymbol{AB} = \boldsymbol{C} = \begin{pmatrix} c_{11} & c_{12} & \cdots & c_{1n} \\ c_{21} & c_{22} & \cdots & c_{2n} \\ \vdots & \vdots & \ddots & \vdots \\ c_{m1} & c_{m2} & \cdots & c_{mn} \end{pmatrix}_{m\times n}, \quad \text{where } c_{ij} = \sum_{k=1}^{r} a_{ik}b_{kj}.$$

Each element of the matrix $\boldsymbol{C}$ is derived as follows:

$$\begin{aligned} c_{11} &= a_{11}b_{11} + a_{12}b_{21} + \cdots + a_{1r}b_{r1} \\ c_{12} &= a_{11}b_{12} + a_{12}b_{22} + \cdots + a_{1r}b_{r2} \\ \vdots \quad & \quad \vdots \qquad\quad \vdots \qquad\qquad\quad \vdots \\ c_{1n} &= a_{11}b_{1n} + a_{12}b_{2n} + \cdots + a_{1r}b_{rn} \\ c_{21} &= a_{21}b_{11} + a_{22}b_{21} + \cdots + a_{2r}b_{r1} \end{aligned}$$

$$c_{22} = a_{21}b_{12} + a_{22}b_{22} + \cdots + a_{2r}b_{r2}$$
$$\vdots \quad \vdots \quad \vdots \quad \vdots$$
$$c_{mn} = a_{m1}b_{1n} + a_{m2}b_{2n} + \cdots + a_{mr}b_{rn}.$$

Note that if the compatibility condition is not satisfied, matrix multiplication cannot be performed.

Example: Let $\boldsymbol{A} = \begin{pmatrix} 3 & 2 & 1 \\ 4 & 5 & 6 \end{pmatrix}$ and $\boldsymbol{B} = \begin{pmatrix} 9 & 10 \\ 12 & 11 \\ 14 & 13 \end{pmatrix}$.

The product of $\boldsymbol{AB} = \boldsymbol{C}$ is given by

$$\boldsymbol{AB} = \boldsymbol{C} = \begin{pmatrix} c_{11} & c_{12} \\ c_{21} & c_{22} \end{pmatrix}_{2\times 2} = \begin{pmatrix} \sum_{k=1}^{3} a_{1k}b_{k1} & \sum_{k=1}^{3} a_{1k}b_{k2} \\ \sum_{k=1}^{3} a_{2k}b_{k1} & \sum_{k=1}^{3} a_{2k}b_{k2} \end{pmatrix}$$
$$= \begin{pmatrix} 65 & 65 \\ 180 & 173 \end{pmatrix}.$$

The product of $\boldsymbol{BA} = \boldsymbol{C}$ is

$$\boldsymbol{BA} = \boldsymbol{C} = \begin{pmatrix} c_{11} & c_{12} & c_{13} \\ c_{21} & c_{22} & c_{23} \\ c_{31} & c_{32} & c_{33} \end{pmatrix} = \begin{pmatrix} 67 & 68 & 69 \\ 80 & 79 & 78 \\ 94 & 93 & 92 \end{pmatrix}.$$

1.2.3 *Laws of matrix operations*

1.2.3.1 *Laws of matrix addition*

Matrix addition (and subtraction) is both associative and commutative.

- Associative law: $(\boldsymbol{A} \pm \boldsymbol{B}) \pm \boldsymbol{C} = \boldsymbol{A} \pm (\boldsymbol{B} \pm \boldsymbol{C})$.
- Commutative law: $\boldsymbol{A} \pm \boldsymbol{B} = \boldsymbol{B} \pm \boldsymbol{A}$.

1.2.3.2 *Laws of matrix multiplication*

Matrix multiplication is associative but not commutative.

- Associative law: $(\boldsymbol{AB})\boldsymbol{C} = \boldsymbol{A}(\boldsymbol{BC}) = \boldsymbol{ABC}$.

This holds provided that the compatibility condition between adjacent matrices is satisfied.

For example, $\boldsymbol{A}_{m\times n}\ \boldsymbol{B}_{n\times p}\ \boldsymbol{C}_{p\times k} = \boldsymbol{D}_{m\times k}$.

- Not commutative: $\boldsymbol{AB} \neq \boldsymbol{BA}$ (even if the compatibility condition is met).

For example, if $\boldsymbol{A} = \begin{pmatrix} 1 & 2 \\ 3 & 4 \end{pmatrix}$ and $\boldsymbol{B} = \begin{pmatrix} -1 & 0 \\ 2 & 3 \end{pmatrix}$, then $\boldsymbol{AB} = \begin{pmatrix} 3 & 6 \\ 5 & 12 \end{pmatrix}$ but $\boldsymbol{BA} = \begin{pmatrix} -1 & -2 \\ 11 & 16 \end{pmatrix}$.

Note here that scalars are commutative in multiplication. Thus letting α and β be scalars, we have $\alpha(\beta\boldsymbol{A}) = (\alpha\beta)\boldsymbol{A} = \beta(\alpha\boldsymbol{A})$.

- Distributive law of matrix multiplication over matrix addition:

$$\boldsymbol{A}(\boldsymbol{B} \pm \boldsymbol{C}) = \boldsymbol{AB} \pm \boldsymbol{AC}$$

$$(\boldsymbol{B} \pm \boldsymbol{C})\boldsymbol{A} = \boldsymbol{BA} \pm \boldsymbol{CA}.$$

In the first case, we pre-multiply the sum (difference) of two matrices $\boldsymbol{B}$ and $\boldsymbol{C}$ by another matrix $\boldsymbol{A}$. In the second case, we post-multiply the sum (difference) of the two matrices by $\boldsymbol{A}$. Note again that $\boldsymbol{A}(\boldsymbol{B} \pm \boldsymbol{C})$ is generally not equal to $(\boldsymbol{B} \pm \boldsymbol{C})\boldsymbol{A}$, as matrix multiplication is not commutative.

1.2.4 *Special types of matrices*

1.2.4.1 *Identity matrix*

One special type of matrix is the identity matrix. This matrix is square, meaning that it has the same number of rows and columns.

Its diagonal elements (from top left to bottom right) are all equal to one, while all other (off-diagonal) elements are zeros. Identity matrices are typically denoted as $\boldsymbol{I}_n = (\delta_{ij})_{n\times n}$, where $\delta_{ij} = 1$ for $i = j$ and $\delta_{ij} = 0$ for $i \neq j$. The subscript n indicates the size of the matrix, as in $\boldsymbol{I}_n$.

$$\boldsymbol{I}_2 = \begin{pmatrix} 1 & 0 \\ 0 & 1 \end{pmatrix}, \quad \boldsymbol{I}_3 = \begin{pmatrix} 1 & 0 & 0 \\ 0 & 1 & 0 \\ 0 & 0 & 1 \end{pmatrix}, \quad \boldsymbol{I}_4 = \begin{pmatrix} 1 & 0 & 0 & 0 \\ 0 & 1 & 0 & 0 \\ 0 & 0 & 1 & 0 \\ 0 & 0 & 0 & 1 \end{pmatrix}.$$

Properties of the identity matrix:

1. $\boldsymbol{I}_n\boldsymbol{A} = \boldsymbol{A}\boldsymbol{I}_n = \boldsymbol{A}$, where $\boldsymbol{A}$ is any $n \times n$ matrix.
2. $\boldsymbol{AIB} = \boldsymbol{AB}\ \forall\ \boldsymbol{A}$ and $\boldsymbol{B}$.

Let $\boldsymbol{I}_2 = \begin{pmatrix} 1 & 0 \\ 0 & 1 \end{pmatrix}$, $\boldsymbol{A} = \begin{pmatrix} 1 & 2 \\ 3 & 4 \end{pmatrix}$, $\boldsymbol{B} = \begin{pmatrix} 5 & 4 \\ 0 & 1 \end{pmatrix}$, then $\boldsymbol{AB} = \begin{pmatrix} 5 & 6 \\ 15 & 16 \end{pmatrix}$, and from the aforementioned first property, we have $\boldsymbol{AI}_2 = \boldsymbol{A}$ and $\boldsymbol{I}_2\boldsymbol{B} = \boldsymbol{B}$; thus $\boldsymbol{AIB} = \boldsymbol{AB} = \begin{pmatrix} 5 & 6 \\ 15 & 16 \end{pmatrix}$.

1.2.4.2 *Null matrix*

Another special type of matrix is the null matrix, which is also known as the zero matrix. All elements in this matrix are scalar zeros. The null matrix is denoted as $\mathbf{0} = (a_{ij})$, where $a_{ij} = 0\ \forall\ i, j$. Null matrices can be non-square, unlike identity matrices. For example,

$$\mathbf{0}_{2\times 2} = \begin{pmatrix} 0 & 0 \\ 0 & 0 \end{pmatrix}, \quad \mathbf{0}_{2\times 3} = \begin{pmatrix} 0 & 0 & 0 \\ 0 & 0 & 0 \end{pmatrix}.$$

Properties of the null matrix:

1. $\boldsymbol{A} \pm \mathbf{0} = \boldsymbol{A}$, where $\boldsymbol{A}$ and $\mathbf{0}$ are of the same dimension.
2. $\boldsymbol{A} - \boldsymbol{A} = \mathbf{0}$, where $\mathbf{0}$ has the same dimension as $\boldsymbol{A}$.

Note that if $\boldsymbol{AB} = \mathbf{0}$, it does not necessarily imply that either $\boldsymbol{A}$ or $\boldsymbol{B}$ is itself a zero matrix. That is, $\boldsymbol{AB} = \mathbf{0} \nRightarrow \boldsymbol{A} = \mathbf{0}$ or $\boldsymbol{B} = \mathbf{0}$. For instance, let $\boldsymbol{A} = \begin{pmatrix} 1 & 1 & 1 \\ 1 & 1 & 1 \end{pmatrix}$ and let $\boldsymbol{B} = \begin{pmatrix} 1 & 1 & -2 \\ 1 & -2 & 1 \\ -2 & 1 & 1 \end{pmatrix}$. We find that $\boldsymbol{AB} = \mathbf{0}_{2\times 3}$. That is,

$$\boldsymbol{AB} = \begin{pmatrix} 1 & 1 & 1 \\ 1 & 1 & 1 \end{pmatrix} \begin{pmatrix} 1 & 1 & -2 \\ 1 & -2 & 1 \\ -2 & 1 & 1 \end{pmatrix} = \begin{pmatrix} 0 & 0 & 0 \\ 0 & 0 & 0 \end{pmatrix} = \mathbf{0}_{2\times 3}.$$

However, the product of $\boldsymbol{BA}$ cannot be defined because the compatibility condition is not satisfied.

1.2.5 *Transpose of a matrix*

To obtain the transpose of a matrix $\boldsymbol{A}$ of dimension $m \times n$, usually denoted as $\boldsymbol{A}^T$ or $\boldsymbol{A}'$, we take the rows of $\boldsymbol{A}$ and turn them into columns. Thus, the transpose is given by $\boldsymbol{A}^T = (a_{ji})_{n\times m}$. Conversely, to transpose $\boldsymbol{A}^T$ back to $\boldsymbol{A}$, we take the columns of $\boldsymbol{A}^T$ and turn them into rows.

Definition: $\boldsymbol{B} = (b_{ij})_{n\times m}$ is the transpose of $\boldsymbol{A} = (a_{ij})_{m\times n}$ if

$$a_{ji} = b_{ij} \ \forall\ i = 1, \ldots, n \text{ and } j = 1, \ldots, m.$$

Example:

$$\boldsymbol{A} = \begin{pmatrix} 1 & 2 & 3 \\ a & b & c \\ -4 & -5 & -6 \\ x & y & z \end{pmatrix} \Rightarrow \boldsymbol{A}^T = \begin{pmatrix} 1 & a & -4 & x \\ 2 & b & -5 & y \\ 3 & c & -6 & z \end{pmatrix}.$$

Properties of transposes:

(1) $(\boldsymbol{A}^T)^T = \boldsymbol{A}$. The transpose of the transpose is the original matrix.
(2) $(\boldsymbol{A} \pm \boldsymbol{B})^T = \boldsymbol{A}^T \pm \boldsymbol{B}^T$. If $\boldsymbol{A}$ and $\boldsymbol{B}$ are of the same dimensions, the transpose of a sum (or difference) of matrices is the sum (or difference) of their individual transposes.
(3) $(\theta \boldsymbol{A})^T = \theta \boldsymbol{A}^T$, where θ is a real number.
(4) $(\boldsymbol{AB})^T = \boldsymbol{B}^T \boldsymbol{A}^T$. The transpose of the product of two matrices is the product of their individual transposes in reverse order.

We now introduce three additional types of matrices: the symmetric matrix, the anti-symmetric matrix, and the orthogonal matrix. They can be defined as follows.

Definition: Symmetric matrix
A matrix $\boldsymbol{A} = (a_{ij})$ of dimension $n \times n$ (a square matrix) is symmetric if and only if transposing gives $\boldsymbol{A}^T = \boldsymbol{A}$, which means that $a_{ij} = a_{ji} \ \forall \ i \,\text{and}\, j$.

Definition: Anti-symmetric matrix
A square matrix $\boldsymbol{A} = (a_{ij})_{n \times n}$ is said to be anti-symmetric if transposing gives $a_{ij} = -a_{ji} \ \forall \ i \,\text{and}\, j$. This can be expressed as $\boldsymbol{A} = -\boldsymbol{A}^T$.

Definition: Orthogonal matrix
A square matrix $\boldsymbol{A} = (a_{ij})_{n \times n}$ is said to be orthogonal if and only if $\boldsymbol{A}^T \boldsymbol{A} = \boldsymbol{A}\boldsymbol{A}^T = \boldsymbol{I}$, where $\boldsymbol{I}$ is the identity matrix.

1.2.6 *Inverse matrix*

Definition: Let $\boldsymbol{A}$ be an $n \times n$ square matrix. An $n \times n$ matrix $\boldsymbol{B}$ is called the inverse of $\boldsymbol{A}$ if and only if $\boldsymbol{AB} = \boldsymbol{BA} = \boldsymbol{I}$. Thus, the inverse matrix $\boldsymbol{A}^{-1}$ of dimension $n \times n$ is defined as $\boldsymbol{A}^{-1}\boldsymbol{A} = \boldsymbol{A}\boldsymbol{A}^{-1} = \boldsymbol{I}$.

Example: Given $\boldsymbol{A} = \begin{pmatrix} 1 & 2 \\ 3 & 4 \end{pmatrix}$, find $\boldsymbol{A}^{-1}$.

Let $\boldsymbol{A}^{-1} = \begin{pmatrix} a & b \\ c & d \end{pmatrix}$. We know from the earlier definition that $\boldsymbol{A}\boldsymbol{A}^{-1} = \boldsymbol{I}$, where $\boldsymbol{I} = \begin{pmatrix} 1 & 0 \\ 0 & 1 \end{pmatrix}$. This leads to the equation $\begin{pmatrix} 1 & 2 \\ 3 & 4 \end{pmatrix}\begin{pmatrix} a & b \\ c & d \end{pmatrix} = \begin{pmatrix} 1 & 0 \\ 0 & 1 \end{pmatrix}$. By performing the matrix multiplication on the left-hand side, we obtain

$$\begin{pmatrix} a + 2c & b + 2d \\ 3a + 4c & 3b + 4d \end{pmatrix} = \begin{pmatrix} 1 & 0 \\ 0 & 1 \end{pmatrix}.$$

We therefore have a system of four equations with four unknowns

$$a + 2c = 1$$

$$b + 2d = 0$$

$$3a + 4c = 0$$

$$3b + 4d = 1.$$

Solving this system yields

$$\boldsymbol{A}^{-1} = \begin{pmatrix} -2 & 1 \\ 3/2 & -1/2 \end{pmatrix}.$$

We note that a matrix can have an inverse only if it is square. This means that being square is a necessary condition for a matrix to be invertible. However, not all square matrices have inverses. A square matrix that has an inverse is called *non-singular* (or regular), while a square matrix that does not have an inverse is referred to as *singular*. If a matrix does have an inverse, that inverse is unique.

Properties of inverse matrices:

(1) $(\boldsymbol{A}^{-1})^{-1} = \boldsymbol{A}$. The inverse of an inverse matrix is the original matrix.
(2) For any scalar μ, with $\mu \neq 0$, $(\mu\boldsymbol{A})^{-1} = \frac{1}{\mu}\boldsymbol{A}^{-1}$.
(3) If the matrices $\boldsymbol{A}$ and $\boldsymbol{B}$ are both non-singular (i.e., $\boldsymbol{A}^{-1}$ and $\boldsymbol{B}^{-1}$ exist) and of the same dimension, then $(\boldsymbol{AB})^{-1} = \boldsymbol{B}^{-1}\boldsymbol{A}^{-1}$.
(4) For any invertible matrix $\boldsymbol{A}$, we have $(\boldsymbol{A}^T)^{-1} = (\boldsymbol{A}^{-1})^T$, which means that the inverse of the transpose is equal to the transpose of the inverse.

1.2.7 *Determinants*

Consider a 2×2 matrix $\boldsymbol{A} = \begin{pmatrix} a_{11} & a_{12} \\ a_{21} & a_{22} \end{pmatrix}$. The determinant of $\boldsymbol{A}$, denoted by $\det(\boldsymbol{A})$ or $|\boldsymbol{A}|$, is a scalar value computed from the entries of the matrix. Determinants are defined only for square matrices. In the case of a 2×2 matrix, the determinant is given by

$$\det(\boldsymbol{A}) = |\boldsymbol{A}| = a_{11}a_{22} - a_{12}a_{21},$$

which is computed as the difference between the product of the elements on the main diagonal and the product of the other two elements.

1.2.7.1 *Minors*

Definition: Let $\boldsymbol{A}$ be a square matrix of dimension $n \times n$. Let $\boldsymbol{A}_{ij}$ be the resulting $(n-1)\times(n-1)$ submatrix obtained when row i and column j are deleted from $\boldsymbol{A}$. The scalar M_{ij}, where $M_{ij} = |\boldsymbol{A}_{ij}|$, is called the (i, j)th minor of matrix $\boldsymbol{A}$.

Example:

Original matrix $\boldsymbol{A}_{3\times 3}$	Crossing out all entries in row 1 and column 1	The resulting minor M_{11}
$\boldsymbol{A} = \begin{pmatrix} a_{11} & a_{12} & a_{13} \\ a_{21} & a_{22} & a_{23} \\ a_{31} & a_{32} & a_{33} \end{pmatrix}$	$\begin{pmatrix} a_{11} & a_{12} & a_{13} \\ a_{21} & a_{22} & a_{23} \\ a_{31} & a_{32} & a_{33} \end{pmatrix}$	$\begin{vmatrix} a_{22} & a_{23} \\ a_{32} & a_{33} \end{vmatrix} = a_{22}a_{33} - a_{32}a_{23}$

1.2.7.2 *Cofactors*

Definition: For an $n \times n$ square matrix $\boldsymbol{A}$, the cofactor C_{ij} is defined as $C_{ij} = (-1)^{i+j} M_{ij}$.

From this definition, the distribution of the positive and negative signs for a cofactor matrix of dimension 3×3 is as follows:

$$\begin{pmatrix} + & - & + \\ - & + & - \\ + & - & + \end{pmatrix}.$$

Example: Let $\boldsymbol{B} = \begin{pmatrix} 4 & 2 & 3 \\ 0 & 7 & 6 \\ 1 & 8 & 9 \end{pmatrix}$. Matrix $\boldsymbol{B}$ is of the form $\boldsymbol{B} = \begin{pmatrix} a_{11} & a_{12} & a_{13} \\ a_{21} & a_{22} & a_{23} \\ a_{31} & a_{32} & a_{33} \end{pmatrix}$ with the corresponding cofactor matrix given by $\begin{pmatrix} C_{11} & C_{12} & C_{13} \\ C_{21} & C_{22} & C_{23} \\ C_{31} & C_{32} & C_{33} \end{pmatrix}$. The following table illustrates how to calculate the elements of the cofactor matrix.

Minor M_{11}	Cofactor operation	Cofactor operation	The resulting cofactor C_{11}
$\begin{vmatrix} a_{22} & a_{23} \\ a_{32} & a_{33} \end{vmatrix}$	$C_{11} = (-1)^{1+1} M_{11}$	$C_{11} = (-1)^2 \begin{vmatrix} a_{22} & a_{23} \\ a_{32} & a_{33} \end{vmatrix}$	$C_{11} = \begin{vmatrix} a_{22} & a_{23} \\ a_{32} & a_{33} \end{vmatrix} = a_{22}a_{33} - a_{32}a_{23}$

Minor M_{32}	Cofactor operation	Cofactor operation	The resulting cofactor C_{32}
$\begin{vmatrix} 4 & 3 \\ 0 & 6 \end{vmatrix}$	$C_{32} = (-1)^{3+2} M_{32}$	$C_{32} = (-1)^5 \begin{vmatrix} 4 & 3 \\ 0 & 6 \end{vmatrix}$	$C_{32} = -24$

It follows that the cofactor matrix of $\boldsymbol{B}$ is

$$\begin{pmatrix} 15 & 6 & -7 \\ 6 & 33 & -30 \\ -9 & -24 & 28 \end{pmatrix}.$$

1.2.7.3 *Adjoint (adjugate) of a matrix*

The adjoint matrix is the transposed matrix of the cofactor matrix. The adjoint of a matrix is usually denoted as Adj.

Example: The adjoint matrices for matrices $\boldsymbol{A}$ and $\boldsymbol{B}$ used in the previous examples are given by

$$\text{Adj}\boldsymbol{A} = \begin{pmatrix} C_{11} & C_{21} & C_{31} \\ C_{12} & C_{22} & C_{32} \\ C_{13} & C_{23} & C_{33} \end{pmatrix} \quad \text{Adj}\boldsymbol{B} = \begin{pmatrix} 15 & 6 & -9 \\ 6 & 33 & -24 \\ -7 & -30 & 28 \end{pmatrix}.$$

Definition: Let $\boldsymbol{A}$ be an $n \times n$ matrix, and let $\boldsymbol{A}_{ij}$ be the $(n-1) \times (n-1)$ matrix obtained from $\boldsymbol{A}$ after deleting the ith row and jth column. The determinant of $\boldsymbol{A}_{ij}$, denoted as $M_{ij} = |\boldsymbol{A}_{ij}|$, is the (i, j)th minor of $\boldsymbol{A}$. The cofactor is defined as $C_{ij} = (-1)^{i+j} M_{ij}$.

The determinant of matrix $\boldsymbol{A}$ by expansion along the first row is given by

$$\begin{aligned}\det\boldsymbol{A} = |\boldsymbol{A}| &= a_{11}M_{11} - a_{12}M_{12} + a_{13}M_{13} + \cdots \\ &\quad + (-1)^{1+n}a_{1n}M_{1n} \\ &= a_{11}C_{11} + a_{12}C_{12} + a_{13}C_{13} + \cdots + a_{1n}C_{1n}.\end{aligned}$$

The general form of $\det\boldsymbol{A}$ for an $n \times n$ matrix $\boldsymbol{A}$ is as follows:

(1) For $n = 1$, $|\boldsymbol{A}| = a_{11}$.
(2) For $n \geq 2$, $|\boldsymbol{A}| = \sum_{j=1}^{n} a_{1j}(-1)^{1+j}M_{1j} = \sum_{j=1}^{n} a_{1j}C_{1j}$.

Note that selecting the first row for expansion in the above-mentioned definitions is arbitrary. In general, for any square matrix $\boldsymbol{A}$, the determinant can be computed by multiplying the entries of any row (or column) by their corresponding cofactors and summing the resulting products

$$|\boldsymbol{A}| = \sum_{j=1}^{n} a_{ij}(-1)^{i+j}M_{ij} = \sum_{j=1}^{n} a_{ij}C_{ij},$$

which can be expressed as

$$|\boldsymbol{A}| = a_{i1}C_{i1} + a_{i2}C_{i2} + \cdots + a_{in}C_{in} \text{ (expansion along row } i)$$

or

$$|\boldsymbol{A}| = a_{1j}C_{1j} + a_{2j}C_{2j} + \cdots + + a_{nj}C_{nj} \text{ (expansion along column } j).$$

Thus, we can select any row or column of a matrix to find its determinant using cofactor expansion.

It should be noted that a matrix has an inverse if and only if its determinant is non-zero. In other words, a non-zero determinant is both a necessary and sufficient condition for the matrix to have an inverse.

1.2.7.4 *Evaluating a second-order determinant*

Let $\boldsymbol{A}$ be a matrix of dimension 2×2

$$\boldsymbol{A} = \begin{pmatrix} a_{11} & a_{12} \\ a_{21} & a_{22} \end{pmatrix}.$$

We say that $\boldsymbol{A}$ is non-singular if and only if $\det(\boldsymbol{A}) = |\boldsymbol{A}| = a_{11}a_{22} - a_{12}a_{21} \neq 0$. Applying the definition given earlier, we can express the determinant as $|\boldsymbol{A}| = a_{11}\det(a_{22}) - a_{12}\det(a_{21})$, where the first term, $a_{11}\det(a_{22})$, represents the first element of the first row (a_{11}) of matrix $\boldsymbol{A}$ multiplied by the determinant of the sub-matrix obtained by deleting the row and the column containing that element (i.e., deleting the first row and the first column of matrix $\boldsymbol{A}$). Similarly, the second term, $a_{12}\det(a_{21})$, corresponds to the second element of the first row (a_{12}) of matrix $\boldsymbol{A}$ multiplied by the determinant of the sub-matrix obtained by deleting the row and the column containing that element (i.e., deleting the first row and the second column of matrix $\boldsymbol{A}$). We can write this in more general form as

$$|\boldsymbol{A}| = a_{11}M_{11} - a_{12}M_{12} = a_{11}C_{11} + a_{12}C_{12} = a_{11}a_{22} - a_{12}a_{21}.$$

Example: Let $\boldsymbol{A} = \begin{pmatrix} a & b \\ c & d \end{pmatrix}$. Then $|\boldsymbol{A}| = \begin{vmatrix} a & b \\ c & d \end{vmatrix} = ad - bc.$

1.2.7.5 *Evaluating a higher-order determinant*

Let $\boldsymbol{A}$ be a square matrix of dimension 3×3

$$\boldsymbol{A} = \begin{pmatrix} a_{11} & a_{12} & a_{13} \\ a_{21} & a_{22} & a_{23} \\ a_{31} & a_{32} & a_{33} \end{pmatrix}.$$

The determinant of matrix $\boldsymbol{A}$, when expanded along the first row, is given by

$$\begin{aligned}\det(\boldsymbol{A}) = |\boldsymbol{A}| &= a_{11}C_{11} + a_{12}C_{12} + a_{13}C_{13} \\ &= a_{11}M_{11} - a_{12}M_{12} + a_{13}M_{13} \\ &= a_{11}\begin{vmatrix} a_{22} & a_{23} \\ a_{32} & a_{33} \end{vmatrix} - a_{12}\begin{vmatrix} a_{21} & a_{23} \\ a_{31} & a_{33} \end{vmatrix} + a_{13}\begin{vmatrix} a_{21} & a_{22} \\ a_{31} & a_{32} \end{vmatrix}.\end{aligned}$$

The explanation for the first, second, and third terms on the right-hand side of the equation is similar to the explanation provided earlier for the 2×2 matrix. More generally, the j-th term on the right-hand side is given by a_{1j} multiplied by the determinant of the submatrix obtained by deleting the first row and j-th column from matrix $\boldsymbol{A}$.

Example: Let $\boldsymbol{A} = \begin{pmatrix} 1 & 5 & 7 \\ 1 & 3 & 7 \\ 0 & 0 & 4 \end{pmatrix}$. The determinant of $\boldsymbol{A}$, when expanded along the first row, is given by

$$\begin{aligned}|\boldsymbol{A}| &= a_{11}\begin{vmatrix} a_{22} & a_{23} \\ a_{32} & a_{33} \end{vmatrix} - a_{12}\begin{vmatrix} a_{21} & a_{23} \\ a_{31} & a_{33} \end{vmatrix} + a_{13}\begin{vmatrix} a_{21} & a_{22} \\ a_{31} & a_{32} \end{vmatrix} \\ &= 1\begin{vmatrix} 3 & 7 \\ 0 & 4 \end{vmatrix} - 5\begin{vmatrix} 1 & 7 \\ 0 & 4 \end{vmatrix} + 7\begin{vmatrix} 1 & 3 \\ 0 & 0 \end{vmatrix} = -8.\end{aligned}$$

It is worth noting that we can also evaluate the determinant of matrix $\boldsymbol{A}$ by using cofactor expansion along the third row instead of the first row shown earlier. This approach has the advantage of involving fewer calculations, given that the elements a_{31} and a_{32} are equal to zero. Indeed, it is straightforward to confirm that $|\boldsymbol{A}| = 0 - 0 + 4(1 \cdot 3 - 1 \cdot 5) = -8$.

1.3 Further Exercises and Applications

(1.1) If the inverse of a matrix $\boldsymbol{A}$ exists, then $\boldsymbol{A}$ is a square matrix. We can state two conditions as follows:

$$\text{Condition } p\text{: } \boldsymbol{A}^{-1} \text{ exists}$$

$$\text{Condition } q\text{: } \boldsymbol{A} \text{ is a square matrix}$$

(a) Is q a necessary or sufficient condition for p?
(b) Does condition p or q suggest a stricter requirement?

Solution:

(a) Condition q is necessary for p. This means that not all matrices have inverses; a matrix has an inverse only if it is square. Therefore, if $\boldsymbol{A}^{-1}$ exists (condition p), it follows that $\boldsymbol{A}$ must be a square matrix (condition q).
(b) Condition p suggests a stricter requirement than q, because if condition p holds (i.e., the inverse exists), then condition q must also hold (i.e., the matrix must be square).

(1.2) Matrix addition and subtraction.

$$\text{Given } \boldsymbol{A}_{4\times 4} = \begin{pmatrix} 1 & 3 & 19 & 2 \\ 14 & 8 & 0 & -4 \\ 2 & 1 & 9 & 7 \\ 11 & 8 & 6 & -5 \end{pmatrix} \quad \text{and}$$

$$\boldsymbol{B}_{4\times 4} = \begin{pmatrix} 11 & 1 & 9 & 2 \\ 4 & 8 & 10 & -4 \\ 7 & 11 & 16 & 14 \\ 22 & 16 & 12 & -10 \end{pmatrix},$$

find $\boldsymbol{C}_{4\times 4} = \boldsymbol{A}_{4\times 4} + \boldsymbol{B}_{4\times 4}$ and $\boldsymbol{D}_{4\times 4} = \boldsymbol{A}_{4\times 4} - \boldsymbol{B}_{4\times 4}$.

Solution:

Summation of $\boldsymbol{A}_{4\times4} + \boldsymbol{B}_{4\times4} = \boldsymbol{C}_{4\times4}$ gives us

$$\boldsymbol{A}_{4\times4} + \boldsymbol{B}_{4\times4} = \boldsymbol{C}_{4\times4} = \begin{pmatrix} c_{11} & c_{12} & c_{13} & c_{14} \\ c_{21} & c_{22} & c_{23} & c_{24} \\ c_{31} & c_{32} & c_{33} & c_{34} \\ c_{41} & c_{42} & c_{43} & c_{44} \end{pmatrix}$$

$$= \begin{pmatrix} a_{11}+b_{11} & a_{12}+b_{12} & a_{13}+b_{13} & a_{14}+b_{14} \\ a_{21}+b_{21} & a_{22}+b_{22} & a_{23}+b_{23} & a_{24}+b_{24} \\ a_{31}+b_{31} & a_{32}+b_{32} & a_{33}+b_{33} & a_{34}+b_{34} \\ a_{41}+b_{41} & a_{42}+b_{42} & a_{43}+b_{43} & a_{44}+b_{44} \end{pmatrix}$$

$$= \begin{pmatrix} 12 & 4 & 28 & 4 \\ 18 & 16 & 10 & -8 \\ 9 & 12 & 25 & 21 \\ 33 & 24 & 18 & -15 \end{pmatrix}.$$

Subtraction of $\boldsymbol{A}_{4\times4} - \boldsymbol{B}_{4\times4} = \boldsymbol{D}_{4\times4}$ leads to

$$\boldsymbol{A}_{4\times4} - \boldsymbol{B}_{4\times4} = \boldsymbol{D}_{4\times4} = \begin{pmatrix} d_{11} & d_{12} & d_{13} & d_{14} \\ d_{21} & d_{22} & d_{23} & d_{24} \\ d_{31} & d_{32} & d_{33} & d_{34} \\ d_{41} & d_{42} & d_{43} & d_{44} \end{pmatrix}$$

$$= \begin{pmatrix} a_{11}-b_{11} & a_{12}-b_{12} & a_{13}-b_{13} & a_{14}-b_{14} \\ a_{21}-b_{21} & a_{22}-b_{22} & a_{23}-b_{23} & a_{24}-b_{24} \\ a_{31}-b_{31} & a_{32}-b_{32} & a_{33}-b_{33} & a_{34}-b_{34} \\ a_{41}-b_{41} & a_{42}-b_{42} & a_{43}-b_{43} & a_{44}-b_{44} \end{pmatrix}$$

$$= \begin{pmatrix} -10 & 2 & 10 & 0 \\ 10 & 0 & -10 & 0 \\ -5 & -10 & -7 & -7 \\ -11 & -8 & -6 & 5 \end{pmatrix}.$$

(1.3) Matrix multiplication.

Let $\boldsymbol{A}_{2\times3} = \begin{pmatrix} 3 & 1 & 2 \\ 5 & 7 & 4 \end{pmatrix}$ and $\boldsymbol{B}_{3\times2} = \begin{pmatrix} 1 & -3 \\ -2 & 4 \\ \frac{1}{2} & 7 \end{pmatrix}$. Matrices $\boldsymbol{C}$ and $\boldsymbol{D}$ are the products of $\boldsymbol{A}$ and $\boldsymbol{B}$. Given that $\boldsymbol{C} = \boldsymbol{AB}$ and $\boldsymbol{D} = \boldsymbol{BA}$, find matrices $\boldsymbol{C}$ and $\boldsymbol{D}$.

Solution:

The product of $\boldsymbol{AB} = \boldsymbol{C}$ is given by

$$\boldsymbol{A}_{2\times3}\boldsymbol{B}_{3\times2} = \boldsymbol{C}_{2\times2} = \begin{pmatrix} c_{11} & c_{12} \\ c_{21} & c_{22} \end{pmatrix}_{2\times2}$$

$$= \begin{pmatrix} \sum_{k=1}^{3} a_{1k}b_{k1} & \sum_{k=1}^{3} a_{1k}b_{k2} \\ \sum_{k=1}^{3} a_{2k}b_{k1} & \sum_{k=1}^{3} a_{2k}b_{k2} \end{pmatrix} = \begin{pmatrix} 2 & 9 \\ -7 & 41 \end{pmatrix}.$$

The product of $\boldsymbol{BA} = \boldsymbol{D}$ is given by

$$\boldsymbol{B}_{3\times2}\boldsymbol{A}_{2\times3} = \boldsymbol{D}_{3\times3} = \begin{pmatrix} d_{11} & d_{12} & d_{13} \\ d_{21} & d_{22} & d_{23} \\ d_{31} & d_{32} & d_{33} \end{pmatrix}_{3\times3}$$

$$= \begin{pmatrix} \sum_{k=1}^{2} b_{1k}a_{k1} & \sum_{k=1}^{2} b_{1k}a_{k2} & \sum_{k=1}^{2} b_{1k}a_{k3} \\ \sum_{k=1}^{2} b_{2k}a_{k1} & \sum_{k=1}^{2} b_{2k}a_{k2} & \sum_{k=1}^{2} b_{2k}a_{k3} \\ \sum_{k=1}^{2} b_{3k}a_{k1} & \sum_{k=1}^{2} b_{3k}a_{k2} & \sum_{k=1}^{2} b_{3k}a_{k3} \end{pmatrix}$$

$$= \begin{pmatrix} -12 & -20 & -10 \\ 14 & 26 & 12 \\ \frac{73}{2} & \frac{99}{2} & 29 \end{pmatrix}.$$

(1.4) This exercise requires finding the inverse of a matrix.

$$\text{Given } \boldsymbol{A} = \begin{pmatrix} 5 & 2 \\ -7 & -3 \end{pmatrix}, \text{ find } \boldsymbol{A}^{-1}.$$

Solution:

Letting $\boldsymbol{A}^{-1} = \begin{pmatrix} x & y \\ z & l \end{pmatrix}$ and substituting into the definition of an inverse matrix, we obtain $\begin{pmatrix} 5 & 2 \\ -7 & -3 \end{pmatrix} \begin{pmatrix} x & y \\ z & l \end{pmatrix} = \begin{pmatrix} 1 & 0 \\ 0 & 1 \end{pmatrix}$. This leads to $\begin{pmatrix} 5x+2z & 5y+2l \\ -7x-3z & -7y-3l \end{pmatrix} = \begin{pmatrix} 1 & 0 \\ 0 & 1 \end{pmatrix}$. Thus, we have the following system of equations

$$5x + 2z = 1$$

$$-7x - 3z = 0$$

$$5y + 2l = 0$$

$$-7y - 3l = 1.$$

Solving this system yields

$$\boldsymbol{A}^{-1} = \begin{pmatrix} 3 & 2 \\ -7 & -5 \end{pmatrix}.$$

(1.5) This exercise requires finding the cofactor and the determinant of a matrix.

If $\boldsymbol{A} = \begin{pmatrix} 0 & 6 & 8 \\ 5 & 7 & 9 \\ 6 & 8 & 10 \end{pmatrix}_{3\times 3}$, find the cofactor matrix and the determinant of $\boldsymbol{A}$.

Solution:

Let the cofactor matrix of matrix $\boldsymbol{A}$ be denoted as $\boldsymbol{C_A}$, and let C_{ij} and M_{ij} be the cofactor and the minor of the element a_{ij}, respectively. We obtain

$$\boldsymbol{C_A} = \begin{pmatrix} C_{11} & C_{12} & C_{13} \\ C_{21} & C_{22} & C_{23} \\ C_{31} & C_{32} & C_{33} \end{pmatrix}_{3\times 3}$$

$$= \begin{pmatrix} (-1)^{1+1}M_{11} & (-1)^{1+2}M_{12} & (-1)^{1+3}M_{13} \\ (-1)^{2+1}M_{21} & (-1)^{2+2}M_{22} & (-1)^{2+3}M_{23} \\ (-1)^{3+1}M_{31} & (-1)^{3+2}M_{32} & (-1)^{3+3}M_{33} \end{pmatrix}_{3\times 3}$$

$$= \begin{pmatrix} \begin{vmatrix} 7 & 9 \\ 8 & 10 \end{vmatrix} & -\begin{vmatrix} 5 & 9 \\ 6 & 10 \end{vmatrix} & \begin{vmatrix} 5 & 7 \\ 6 & 8 \end{vmatrix} \\ -\begin{vmatrix} 6 & 8 \\ 8 & 10 \end{vmatrix} & \begin{vmatrix} 0 & 8 \\ 6 & 10 \end{vmatrix} & -\begin{vmatrix} 0 & 6 \\ 6 & 8 \end{vmatrix} \\ \begin{vmatrix} 6 & 8 \\ 7 & 9 \end{vmatrix} & -\begin{vmatrix} 0 & 8 \\ 5 & 9 \end{vmatrix} & \begin{vmatrix} 0 & 6 \\ 5 & 7 \end{vmatrix} \end{pmatrix}_{3\times 3}$$

$$= \begin{pmatrix} -2 & 4 & -2 \\ 4 & -48 & 36 \\ -2 & 40 & -30 \end{pmatrix}_{3\times 3}.$$

The determinant of a matrix can be calculated using cofactor expansion. We can expand along the first row

$$\det \boldsymbol{A} = |\boldsymbol{A}| = \sum_{j=1}^{3} a_{1j}(-1)^{1+j}M_{1j} = \sum_{j=1}^{3} a_{1j}C_{1j} = a_{11}C_{11} + a_{12}C_{12} + a_{13}C_{13}.$$

Substituting a_{1j} and C_{1j}, where $j = 1, 2, 3$, yields

$$\det \boldsymbol{A} = |\boldsymbol{A}| = (0(-2)) + (6 \cdot 4) + (8(-2)) = 0 + 24 - 16 = 8.$$

Note that we can obtain the same result using cofactor expansion along any other row or column of matrix $\boldsymbol{A}$.

(1.6) This exercise involves finding the inverse of a matrix using its adjoint and determinant.

The inverse of a matrix $\boldsymbol{A}$ exists if and only if the determinant of $\boldsymbol{A}$ differs from zero. That is, $\boldsymbol{A}^{-1}$ exists if and only if $|\boldsymbol{A}| \neq 0$. Define the inverse matrix $\boldsymbol{A}^{-1}$ as

$$\boldsymbol{A}^{-1} = \frac{1}{|\boldsymbol{A}|}\text{Adj}\boldsymbol{A}.$$

Given $\boldsymbol{A} = \begin{pmatrix} 3 & 2 \\ 1 & 0 \end{pmatrix}$, find $\boldsymbol{A}^{-1}$.

Solution:

First, note that $|\boldsymbol{A}| = -2 \neq 0$, which implies that $\boldsymbol{A}^{-1}$ exists. To find $\boldsymbol{A}^{-1}$, we use the aforementioned definition. Let

$$\boldsymbol{C} = \begin{pmatrix} C_{11} & C_{12} \\ C_{21} & C_{22} \end{pmatrix} = \begin{pmatrix} 0 & -1 \\ -2 & 3 \end{pmatrix},$$

be the cofactor matrix of $\boldsymbol{A}$. Transposing this we obtain

$$\text{Adj}\boldsymbol{A} = \begin{pmatrix} 0 & -2 \\ -1 & 3 \end{pmatrix}.$$

Substituting into the definition for $\boldsymbol{A}^{-1}$ gives us

$$\boldsymbol{A}^{-1} = \begin{pmatrix} 0 & 1 \\ 1/2 & -3/2 \end{pmatrix}.$$

Further Reading

Bryant, W. D. A. (2023). *Lectures in the Microeconomics of Choice*. Singapore, World Scientific.

Chiang, A. C. & Wainwright, K. (2005). *Fundamental Methods of Mathematical Economics*. Boston, McGraw-Hill.

Horn, R. A. & Johnson, C. R. (1985). *Matrix Analysis*. New York, Cambridge University Press.

Simon, C. P. & Blume, L. (1994). *Mathematics for Economists*. New York, Norton.

CHAPTER 2

DIFFERENTIAL CALCULUS

Learning Objectives

After completing this chapter, students will be able to:

- Understand the concept of a derivative.
- Apply partial differentiation to various functions.
- Derive the total differential and total derivative of a multiple-variable function.
- Apply an implicit function theorem to compute partial derivatives.

This chapter focuses on the study of differential calculus. One of the primary objectives is to find the derivative of a function, a process known as differentiation. The chapter also introduces the concept of the partial derivative, which describes the change in a function with respect to one variable while holding all others constant. Furthermore, the concept of the total derivative is discussed, which is relevant when there is a functional relationship among the independent variables of a function. Total derivatives consider all possible channels — both direct and indirect — through which the effect of an independent variable is transmitted to the dependent variable. Finally, this chapter presents an implicit function theorem and demonstrates how it can be applied to compute partial derivatives, including the slope of an indifference curve and the slope of an isoquant.

2.1 The Concept of Derivative

Assume that there exists a relationship between two variables x and y, which is given by $y = f(x)$. The change in x is the difference between a new value x_1 and the initial value x_0, that is, $x_1 - x_0$. Let the Greek letter Δ (delta) denote this difference (change); thus $\Delta x = x_1 - x_0$ or $x_1 = x_0 + \Delta x$. The corresponding change in the value of the function $y = f(x)$ can be written as $\Delta y = f(x_0 + \Delta x) - f(x_0)$.[1] This indicates the gross or total change in y due to a change in x. The per unit change in y due to a change in x, known as the difference quotient, is given by

$$\frac{\Delta y}{\Delta x} = \frac{f(x_0 + \Delta x) - f(x_0)}{\Delta x}.$$

We are interested in the limit of the difference quotient when Δx approaches infinitesimally small values. Thus, as Δx approaches zero ($\Delta x \to 0$), we take the limit of the difference quotient as follows:

$$\lim_{\Delta x \to 0} \frac{\Delta y}{\Delta x} = \lim_{\Delta x \to 0} \frac{f(x_0 + \Delta x) - f(x_0)}{\Delta x}.$$

[1] $\Delta y = y_1 - y_0 \Leftrightarrow \Delta y = f(x_1) - f(x_0) \Leftrightarrow \Delta y = f(x_0 + \Delta x) - f(x_0)$, given that $x_1 = x_0 + \Delta x$.

If this limit exists, we say that the function $y = f(x)$ is differentiable.

Definition: Let $(x_i, f(x_i))$ be a point on the graph of $y = f(x)$. If the limit, $\lim_{\Delta x \to 0} \frac{\Delta y}{\Delta x}$ exists, the derivative of f at x_i is the slope of the tangent line to the graph of f at $(x_i, f(x_i))$, denoted as

$$\frac{dy}{dx}(x_i) = f'(x_i) = \lim_{\Delta x \to 0} \frac{f(x_i + \Delta x) - f(x_i)}{\Delta x}.$$

Note that continuity is a necessary condition for differentiability, but not a sufficient one. Continuity at a point $x = a$ requires that $\lim_{x \to a} f(x) = f(a)$, which means that the graph of the function f has no breaks at $x = a$. In other words, if a function is differentiable at a point, it must also be continuous at that point. However, the converse does not hold: continuity does not necessarily imply differentiability. For example, the function $f(x) = |x|$ is continuous everywhere, but it is not differentiable at $x = 0$, where the graph has a sharp corner. Another example is $f(x) = x^{1/3}$, which is also continuous everywhere but has a vertical tangent at $x = 0$, so it is not differentiable at that point.[2] These functions are illustrated in Figure 2.1.

2.1.1 *Rules of derivatives for functions with a single variable*

Fundamental functions:

If $f(x) = a$, then $f'(x) = 0$, where a denotes a constant.
If $f(x) = x^a$, then $f'(x) = ax^{a-1}$, where a denotes a constant.

2 At a point where a function has a vertical tangent, the derivative does not exist because the limit of the difference quotient becomes infinite. Since the derivative must be finite to exist, the function is not differentiable at such point.

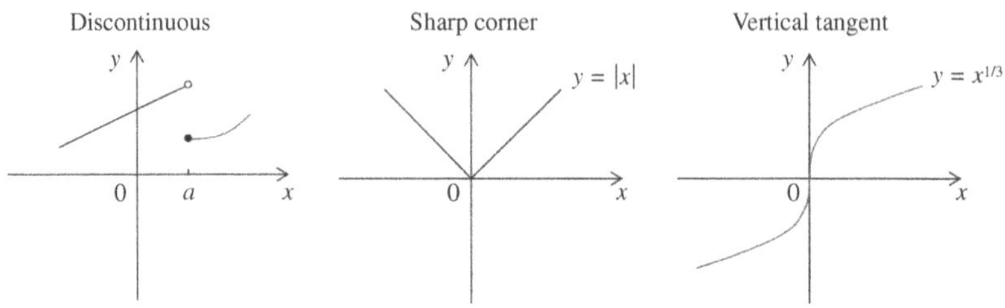

Figure 2.1

If $f(x) = e^x$, then $f'(x) = e^x$.
If $f(x) = \ln x$, then $f'(x) = \frac{1}{x}$, where $x > 0$.
If $f(x) = a^x$, then $f'(x) = a^x \ln a$, where $a > 0$ and $a \neq 1$.
If $f(x) = \log_a x$, then $f'(x) = \frac{1}{x \ln a}$, where $a > 0$ and $a \neq 1$.

Rules of derivatives for the sum, difference, multiplication, and quotient of functions:

If $f(x) = u(x) \pm v(x)$, then $f'(x) = u'(x) \pm v'(x)$.
If $f(x) = \lambda u(x)$, then $f'(x) = \lambda u'(x)$, where λ denotes a constant.
If $f(x) = u(x)v(x)$, then $f'(x) = u'(x)v(x) + u(x)v'(x)$.
If $f(x) = \frac{u(x)}{v(x)}$, then $f'(x) = \frac{u'(x)v(x) - u(x)v'(x)}{(v(x))^2}$, where $v(x) \neq 0$.

Rules of derivatives for composite functions:

If $y = f(z)$, $z = g(x)$, and both $f(z)$ and $g(x)$ are differentiable, then

$$\frac{dy}{dx} = \frac{dy}{dz} \cdot \frac{dz}{dx}.$$

2.2 Differentiation of Functions with Multiple Variables

2.2.1 *Partial differentiation*

Suppose there exists a differentiable function $v = f(x_1, x_2)$ consisting of two independent variables, x_1 and x_2. The derivative of

v with respect to x_1, holding x_2 constant, is known as the partial derivative of v with respect to x_1, and is denoted as[3]

$$f_{x_1}(x_1, x_2), \quad \frac{\partial f(x_1, x_2)}{\partial x_1}, \quad \frac{\partial v}{\partial x_1}.$$

Similarly, the derivative of v with respect to x_2, holding x_1 constant, is referred to as the partial derivative of v with respect to x_2, and is denoted as

$$f_{x_2}(x_1, x_2), \quad \frac{\partial f(x_1, x_2)}{\partial x_2}, \quad \frac{\partial v}{\partial x_2}.$$

More formally, we define

$$f_{x_1}(x_1, x_2) = \lim_{\Delta x_1 \to 0} \frac{f(x_1 + \Delta x_1, x_2) - f(x_1, x_2)}{\Delta x_1},$$

$$f_{x_2}(x_1, x_2) = \lim_{\Delta x_2 \to 0} \frac{f(x_1, x_2 + \Delta x_2) - f(x_1, x_2)}{\Delta x_2},$$

provided that each limit exists.

Example: The partial derivatives of the continuous function $y = f(r, s) = 7r^3 - rs + 3s^2$ are

$$f_r(r, s) \equiv \frac{\partial y}{\partial r} = 21r^2 - s, \quad f_s(r, s) \equiv \frac{\partial y}{\partial s} = -r + 6s.$$

Example: The partial derivatives of the continuous function

$$y = f(u, z) = \frac{u + 2z^2}{3u^2 + 5z}$$

are

$$f_u(u, z) \equiv \frac{\partial y}{\partial u} = \frac{(3u^2 + 5z) - 6u\left(u + 2z^2\right)}{(3u^2 + 5z)^2} = \frac{-3u^2 - 12uz^2 + 5z}{(3u^2 + 5z)^2}$$

$$f_z(u, z) \equiv \frac{\partial y}{\partial z} = \frac{4z\left(3u^2 + 5z\right) - 5\left(u + 2z^2\right)}{(3u^2 + 5z)^2} = \frac{10z^2 + 12u^2 z - 5u}{(3u^2 + 5z)^2}.$$

[3] To differentiate partial from ordinary derivatives, we use the symbol ∂ instead of the Roman letter d. The symbol ∂ is often referred to as "partial d" or "curly d".

2.2.2 *Total differentials and total derivatives*

2.2.2.1 *Total differentials*

Suppose the function $Y = Y(x_1, x_2, \ldots, x_n)$ is continuous and possesses continuous partial derivatives. Suppose further that each x_i is independent of all others. The general form of the total differential of this function is

$$dY = \sum_{i=1}^{n} Y_i dx_i,$$

where $Y_i = \frac{\partial Y}{\partial x_i}$ and $i = 1, 2, \ldots, n$. Accordingly,

$$\begin{aligned} dY &= \frac{\partial Y}{\partial x_1} dx_1 + \frac{\partial Y}{\partial x_2} dx_2 + \cdots + \frac{\partial Y}{\partial x_n} dx_n \\ &= Y_1 dx_1 + Y_2 dx_2 + \cdots + Y_n dx_n. \end{aligned}$$

Example: Suppose that the function

$$Y = Y(x_1,\ x_2,\ x_3,\ x_4) = x_1^2 - 2x_2^3 + 2x_3 x_4^4 - 3x_2 x_3^3 + 5x_1^3 x_4^4$$

is continuous, possesses continuous partial derivatives, and each x_i is independent of all others.

(1) When only one independent variable varies, say x_1, and all other variables are held constant, we obtain

$$dY = \frac{\partial Y}{\partial x_1} dx_1 = (2x_1 + 15x_1^2 x_4^4) dx_1.$$

(2) When some of the independent variables vary, say x_2 and x_3, while all other variables remain constant, we have

$$\begin{aligned} dY &= \frac{\partial Y}{\partial x_2} dx_2 + \frac{\partial Y}{\partial x_3} dx_3 \\ &= -(6x_2^2 + 3x_3^3) dx_2 + (2x_4^4 - 9x_2 x_3^2) dx_3. \end{aligned}$$

(3) When all independent variables vary simultaneously, we obtain

$$\begin{aligned} dY &= \frac{\partial Y}{\partial x_1}dx_1 + \frac{\partial Y}{\partial x_2}dx_2 + \frac{\partial Y}{\partial x_3}dx_3 + \frac{\partial Y}{\partial x_4}dx_4 \\ &= (2x_1 + 15x_1^2x_4^4)dx_1 - (6x_2^2 + 3x_3^3)dx_2 \\ &\quad + (2x_4^4 - 9x_2x_3^2)dx_3 + (8x_3x_4^3 + 20x_1^3x_4^3)dx_4. \end{aligned}$$

2.2.2.2 *Rules of differentials*

Let λ be a constant and $y = A(w, x)$ be a continuously differentiable function, that is, it possesses continuous partial derivatives. Then we have the following rules.

Constant function rule:	$d\lambda = 0$
Power-function rule:	$d(\lambda x^n) = \lambda n x^{n-1}dx$
Sum-difference rule:	$d(w \pm x) = dw \pm dx$
Product rule:	$d(wx) = xdw + wdx$
Quotient rule:	$d\left(\frac{w}{x}\right) = \frac{1}{x^2}(xdw - wdx)$

Example: Let the function $Y = f(r, s) = 7r^3 - rs + 3s^2$ be continuously differentiable everywhere. Let $u = 7r^3$, $w = rs$, and $x = 3s^2$. It follows that

$$d(u \pm w \pm x) = du \pm dw \pm dx.$$

Thus,

$$dY = d(7r^3) - d(rs) + d(3s^2) = (21r^2 - s)dr + (6s - r)ds.$$

2.2.2.3 *Total derivatives*

Consider the continuous function $y = B(x, v)$, where $v = C(x)$. This implies that x affects y not only directly but also indirectly through v. The partial derivative of this function with respect to x only explains the direct effect of x on y, assuming v remains unchanged. In contrast, total derivatives take into account the overall variation in y resulting from a change in x. To obtain the total derivative, we start with the total differential

$$dy = B_x dx + B_v dv.$$

We then divide the total differential by dx

$$\frac{dy}{dx} = B_x + B_v \frac{dv}{dx}.$$

This equation can be rewritten as

$$\frac{dy}{dx} = \underbrace{\frac{\partial y}{\partial x}}_{\text{Direct effect}} + \underbrace{\frac{\partial y}{\partial v}\frac{dv}{dx}}_{\text{Indirect effect}}$$

The first term on the right-hand side represents the direct effect of x on y, whereas the second term represents the indirect effect of x on y through v.

Example: Find the total derivative of the function $y = f(x, w) = 5x^4 + 2x^3 - 3w$ with respect to x, where w is defined as $w = g(x) = x^3 - 7x + 4$.

The total differential of $y = f(x, w)$ is given by

$$dy = f_x dx + f_w dw.$$

Dividing throughout by dx yields

$$\frac{dy}{dx} = f_x + f_w \frac{dw}{dx}.$$

Substitution leads to

$$\frac{dy}{dx} = 20x^3 + 6x^2 - 3(3x^2 - 7) = 20x^3 - 3x^2 + 21.$$

2.2.2.4 *Chain rule for composite functions*

Suppose $y = f(x_1, x_2, \ldots, x_n)$ is a continuous function of n variables $x_1, x_2, \ldots, x_n$ with continuous partial derivatives $\frac{\partial y}{\partial x_1}, \frac{\partial y}{\partial x_2}, \ldots, \frac{\partial y}{\partial x_n}$. If $x_1, x_2, \ldots, x_n$ are differentiable functions of a variable t such that $x_1 = B(t)$, $x_2 = C(t), \ldots, x_n = N(t)$, then the total derivative of y with respect to t is given by

$$\frac{dy}{dt} = \frac{\partial y}{\partial x_1}\frac{dx_1}{dt} + \frac{\partial y}{\partial x_2}\frac{dx_2}{dt} + \cdots + \frac{\partial y}{\partial x_n}\frac{dx_n}{dt}.$$

Similarly, there may be several variables which are functions of different variables. Suppose $y = f(x_1, x_2, \ldots, x_n)$ is a continuous function of n variables, $x_1, x_2, \ldots, x_n$, with continuous partial derivatives, $\frac{\partial y}{\partial x_1}, \frac{\partial y}{\partial x_2}, \ldots, \frac{\partial y}{\partial x_n}$. If $x_1, x_2, \ldots, x_n$ are differentiable functions of k independent variables, $a, b, c, \ldots k$, then

$$\begin{aligned}
\frac{dy}{da} &= \frac{\partial y}{\partial x_1}\frac{\partial x_1}{\partial a} + \frac{\partial y}{\partial x_2}\frac{\partial x_2}{\partial a} + \cdots + \frac{\partial y}{\partial x_n}\frac{\partial x_n}{\partial a} \\
\frac{dy}{db} &= \frac{\partial y}{\partial x_1}\frac{\partial x_1}{\partial b} + \frac{\partial y}{\partial x_2}\frac{\partial x_2}{\partial b} + \cdots + \frac{\partial y}{\partial x_n}\frac{\partial x_n}{\partial b} \\
&\vdots \\
\frac{dy}{dk} &= \frac{\partial y}{\partial x_1}\frac{\partial x_1}{\partial k} + \frac{\partial y}{\partial x_2}\frac{\partial x_2}{\partial k} + \cdots + \frac{\partial y}{\partial x_n}\frac{\partial x_n}{\partial k}.
\end{aligned}$$

Another variation on the current theme is the case where there may be indirect dependencies between only some independent variables of a given function. For example, suppose the function y takes the form $y = f(x_1, x_2, x_3, \ldots, x_n, w, z)$ where $x_1 = B(w, z), x_2 = C(w, z), \ldots, x_n = N(w, z)$. Suppose we want to find the change in y due to a change in w. To this end, we begin by identifying the total differential of y, which is given by

$$dy = f_{x_1}dx_1 + f_{x_2}dx_2 + \cdots + f_{x_n}dx_n + f_w dw + f_z dz.$$

Dividing throughout by dw, we have

$$\frac{dy}{dw} = \frac{\partial y}{\partial x_1}\frac{dx_1}{dw} + \frac{\partial y}{\partial x_2}\frac{dx_2}{dw} + \cdots + \frac{\partial y}{\partial x_n}\frac{dx_n}{dw} + \frac{\partial y}{\partial w}\frac{dw}{dw} + \frac{\partial y}{\partial z}\frac{dz}{dw}.$$

Since we are considering the change in y due to a change in w, z is held constant. The corresponding partial total derivative can be stated as

$$\left.\frac{\partial y}{\partial w}\right|_{z\text{ constant}} = \underbrace{\frac{\partial y}{\partial x_1}\frac{\partial x_1}{\partial w} + \frac{\partial y}{\partial x_2}\frac{\partial x_2}{\partial w} + \cdots + \frac{\partial y}{\partial x_n}\frac{\partial x_n}{\partial w}}_{\text{Indirect effects}} + \underbrace{\frac{\partial y}{\partial w}}_{\text{Direct effect}}.$$

The main idea here is that an independent variable w can influence the dependent variable y through direct and indirect channels. Our analysis has accounted for both of these channels.

2.3 An Implicit Function Theorem

An implicit function theorem provides conditions under which, from a given equation $F(y, x_1, x_2, \ldots, x_n) = 0$, we can obtain an implicit function $y = f(x_1, x_2, \ldots, x_n)$.[4] If the theorem holds, it allows us to calculate partial derivatives, even when it is not possible to solve explicitly $F(y, x_1, x_2, \ldots, x_n) = 0$ for the dependent variable, y.

Theorem: Consider the equation $F(y, x_1, x_2, \ldots, x_n) = 0$. If the following two conditions hold:

(a) F has continuous partial derivatives $\frac{\partial F}{\partial y}, \frac{\partial F}{\partial x_1}, \frac{\partial F}{\partial x_2}, \ldots, \frac{\partial F}{\partial x_n}$.

(b) At a point $(x_{10}, x_{20}, \ldots, x_{n0})$ satisfying $F(y, x_1, x_2, \ldots, x_n) = 0$, we have $\frac{\partial F}{\partial y} \neq 0$.

4 For more information on implicit function theorems, the reader is directed to the discussion in Protter and Morrey (1991).

Then, there exists an implicit function $y = f(x_1, x_2, \ldots, x_n)$ in the neighborhood of the point $(x_{10}, x_{20}, \ldots, x_{n0})$.

If this implicit function theorem holds, partial derivatives can be calculated as follows:

$$\frac{\partial y}{\partial x_i} = -\frac{\frac{\partial F}{\partial x_i}}{\frac{\partial F}{\partial y}} = -\frac{F_{x_i}}{F_y}, \quad \text{for } i = 1, \ldots, n.$$

Example: Consider the equation

$$F(y, w, x, z) = y^3x^3 + y^4w^3 + wxyz + 7xw^3 - 3z^2 - 9 = 0.$$

Calculate the partial derivative $\frac{\partial y}{\partial x}$ at the point $(1, 1, 1, 0)$, where an implicit function may be defined.

This equation cannot be easily solved for y in terms of x, w and z. Thus, to calculate the partial derivative $\frac{\partial y}{\partial x}$, we use the implicit function theorem stated earlier. Accordingly, we can find a point where F_y is non-zero and satisfies the aforementioned equation, given that F_w, F_x, F_y, and F_z are all continuous.

$$\begin{aligned}
F_w &= 3y^4w^2 + xyz + 21xw^2, \\
F_x &= 3y^3x^2 + wyz + 7w^3, \\
F_y &= 3y^2x^3 + 4y^3w^3 + wxz, \\
F_z &= wxy - 6z.
\end{aligned}$$

Note that $F_y = 3y^2x^3 + 4y^3w^3 + wxz \neq 0$ at the point $(1, 1, 1, 0)$, which also satisfies the equation $F(y, w, x, z) = y^3x^3 + y^4w^3 + wxyz + 7xw^3 - 3z^2 - 9 = 0$. Hence, an implicit function of the form $y = f(w, x, z)$ exists around that point. We can then calculate the partial derivative of interest: $\frac{\partial y}{\partial x} = -\frac{F_x}{F_y} = -\frac{3y^3x^2 + wyz + 7w^3}{3y^2x^3 + 4y^3w^3 + wxz}$. Substituting $(1, 1, 1, 0)$, this partial derivative attains the value $-\frac{10}{7}$.

2.4 Further Exercises and Applications

(2.1) Consider the utility function $U = U(x_1, x_2, \ldots, x_n)$, where $x_1, x_2, \ldots, x_n$ denote the amounts of goods $1, 2, \ldots, n$. Let the amounts of all goods vary simultaneously. Find the corresponding change in U.

Solution:

The total differential of the utility function is

$$dU = U_1 dx_1 + U_2 dx_2 + \cdots + U_n dx_n,$$

where $U_i = \frac{\partial U}{\partial x_i}$, for $i = 1, \ldots, n$. This gives us the change in utility when the amounts of all goods vary simultaneously.

(2.2) Let $U = U(x_1, x_2)$ be a continuous utility function which possesses continuous partial derivatives and the amount of good 1, x_1, is independent of the amount of good 2, x_2. Find the slope of an indifference curve.

Solution:

To find the slope of an indifference curve, we vary x_1 and x_2 simultaneously so that utility remains unchanged; that is, we move along an indifference curve. This implies

$$dU = U_1 dx_1 + U_2 dx_2 = 0,$$

which can be rewritten as

$$\frac{dx_2}{dx_1} = -\frac{U_1}{U_2},$$

where U_i is the marginal utility of good $i = 1, 2$. The negative of the ratio of the marginal utilities of the two goods is known as the marginal rate of substitution (MRS) and represents the slope of an indifference curve.

(2.3) Assume that $U(x, y, \bar{u}) = 0$ implicitly defines the indifference curve $x^a + y = \bar{u}$, where $\bar{u}$ is a constant utility level. Find the slope of this indifference curve.

Solution:

The indifference curve $x^a + y = \bar{u}$ is implicitly defined by the equation $U(x, y, \bar{u}) = 0$, so the implicit function theorem holds. Thus, we have

$$\frac{dy}{dx} = -\frac{U_x}{U_y} = -ax^{a-1}.$$

Alternatively, one can calculate the total differential of the utility function $u(x, y) = x^a + y$. Noting that along an indifference curve utility does not change, we have

$$du = u_x dx + u_y dy = 0,$$

which leads to

$$\frac{dy}{dx} = -\frac{u_x}{u_y} = -ax^{a-1}.$$

(2.4) Repeat exercise (2.3) in order to find the slope of an isoquant for the Cobb–Douglas production function $q = Ak^a l^b$, where q is total production, k is the capital input, and l is the labor input.

Solution:

Based on the assumption made in exercise (2.3), the isoquant $Ak^a l^b = \bar{q}$ is implicitly defined by the equation $Q(k, l, \bar{q}) = Ak^a l^b - \bar{q} = 0$, where $\bar{q}$ is a given output level. This implies that the implicit function theorem holds. Thus

$$\frac{dk}{dl} = -\frac{Q_l}{Q_k} = -\frac{bk}{al},$$

where Q_i is the marginal product of input $i = k, l$. The negative of the ratio of the marginal products of the two inputs is known as the marginal rate of technical substitution (MRTS) and represents the slope of an isoquant.

Further Reading

Chiang, A. C. & Wainwright, K. (2005). *Fundamental Methods of Mathematical Economics.* Boston, McGraw-Hill.

Luderer, B., Nollau, V. & Vetters, K. (2009). *Mathematical Formulas for Economists.* Berlin/Heidelberg, Springer Science & Business Media.

Protter, M. H. & Morrey, C. B. (1991). Implicit Function Theorems and Lagrange Multipliers. In: *A First Course in Real Analysis.* Undergraduate Texts in Mathematics. New York, Springer.

Simon, C. P. & Blume, L. (1994). *Mathematics for Economists.* New York, Norton.

Sydsaeter, K., Hammond, P., Seierstad, A. & Strom, A. (2008). *Further Mathematics for Economic Analysis* (second edition). Harlow, Pearson.

CHAPTER 3

CONCAVITY AND CONVEXITY OF FUNCTIONS

Learning Objectives

After completing this chapter, students will be able to:

- Understand the difference between a convex function and a convex set.
- Derive the Hessian matrix and the bordered Hessian matrix.
- Use the Hessian matrix to identify concave and convex functions.
- Use the bordered Hessian matrix to identify quasi-concave and quasi-convex functions.

The present chapter focuses on the shape of functions. In doing so, it aims to take the reader one step closer to the study of optimization problems. An objective is to introduce and discuss the concept of a convex set, which is essential as concave or convex functions typically need their domains to be a convex set. The chapter then describes conditions under which a function is concave or convex. For a function of one variable, a straightforward condition for concavity and convexity is provided by the second derivative, whereas for functions of more than one variable the Hessian matrix is employed. Finally, the notion of concavity and convexity is generalized by describing conditions under which a function is quasi-concave and quasi-convex.[1]

3.1 Convex Sets

We define a convex set. A set is convex if, for any pair of points within the set, the line segment joining these points also lies entirely within the set.

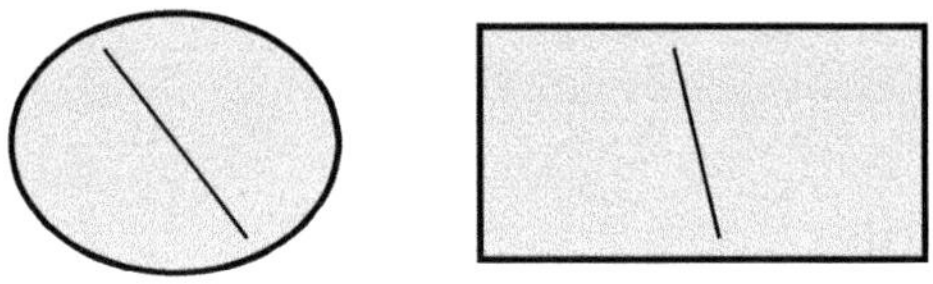

Figure 3.1

More formally, we can state the following two definitions.

Definition: A line segment (x_i, x_j) consists of all points x_k that lie along the straight line connecting the two endpoints x_i and x_j. These points can be expressed as $x_k = \theta x_i + (1 - \theta)x_j$, where $0 \leq \theta \leq 1$.

Definition: A set S is convex if, for any points x_i, $x_j \in S$, the line segment joining x_i and x_j also lies within S. In other words, $\theta x_i + (1 - \theta)x_j \in S$ for any x_i, $x_j \in S$ and $0 \leq \theta \leq 1$.

Figure 3.1 shows an oval and a rectangle. Both shapes are convex sets: the line segment joining any two points within the set lies entirely inside the set, regardless of whether the points are on the boundary or in the interior.

1 The work of Kythe (2018) provides additional insights related to this chapter. Interested readers may refer to the text for further information.

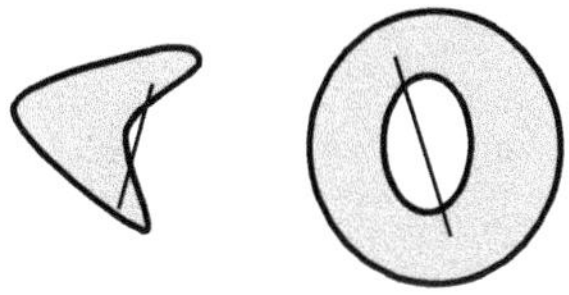

Figure 3.2

In Figure 3.2, the sets are non-convex. For example, the first shape has an indentation, so the line segment joining any two points in the set does not always lie within the set. The second shape, although not indented, contains a hole in the center, which makes it non-convex. Another way to put this is that a convex set cannot have any indentations or holes. For example, the budget line — representing the set of all consumption bundles that cost exactly the consumer's income — divides R^2 into two convex sets: one above the budget line and one below. For any pair of consumption bundles in either set, their linear combination will always result in a line segment that lies entirely within the set.

3.2 Concavity and Convexity

Consider a twice differentiable function of one variable $y = f(x)$. The first derivative dy/dx measures the rate of change or slope of the function. Differentiating the first derivative with respect to x yields the second derivative d^2y/dx^2, which measures the curvature of the function. Note that dy/dx can also be represented using the shorthand notation $f'(x)$, while d^2y/dx^2 can be written as $f''(x)$. If $f'(x) > 0$, we say that the value of the function tends to increase as x increases, whereas if $f'(x) < 0$, the value of the function tends to decrease as x increases. Additionally, if $f''(x) > 0$, the slope of the function tends to increase as x increases, and the opposite is true if $f''(x) < 0$.

3.2.1 *Checking concavity and convexity*

To identify the curvature of a twice differentiable function, that is, whether it is concave or convex, we can use the following sufficient conditions.

- $f(x)$ is convex if $f''(x) \geq 0$ for all points in the domain.
- $f(x)$ is concave if $f''(x) \leq 0$ for all points in the domain.

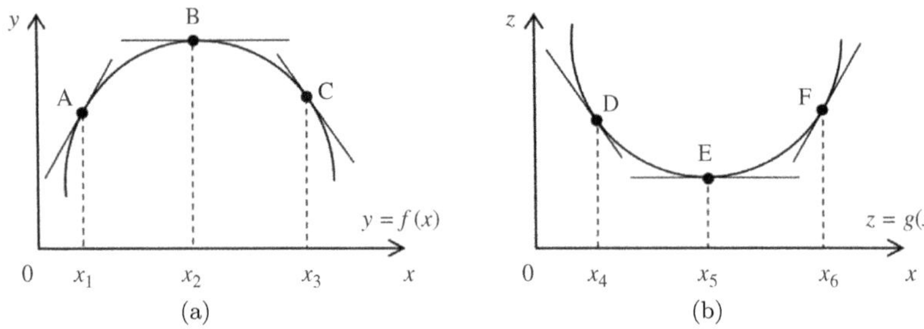

Figure 3.3

For the six points — A, B, C, D, E, and F — shown in Figures 3.3(a) and 3.3(b), the first and second derivative signs are as follows.

At	Derivative signs are		Illustrated by
$x = x_1$	$f'(x_1) > 0$	$f''(x_1) < 0$	Point A
$x = x_2$	$f'(x_2) = 0$	$f''(x_2) < 0$	Point B
$x = x_3$	$f'(x_3) < 0$	$f''(x_3) < 0$	Point C
$x = x_4$	$g'(x_4) < 0$	$g''(x_4) > 0$	Point D
$x = x_5$	$g'(x_5) = 0$	$g''(x_5) > 0$	Point E
$x = x_6$	$g'(x_6) > 0$	$g''(x_6) > 0$	Point F

As the table shows, negative second derivatives (the first three cases) indicate an inverse U-shaped curve, because the slope of the curve decreases as x increases. By contrast, a positive second derivative (the last three cases) suggests that the slope of the curve increases as x increases, meaning that the curve is U-shaped. In other words, the function $y = f(x)$ is concave, whereas the function $z = g(x)$ is convex.

Example: Consider the function $y = f(x) = 5x^2 - x + 3$. Is the graph of y concave or convex?

We begin by calculating the first derivative of y

$$\frac{dy}{dx} = 10x - 1.$$

Next, we calculate the second derivative

$$\frac{d^2y}{dx^2} = 10.$$

The second derivative is positive, and thus the graph of y is convex.

Although concavity and convexity suffice for describing the curvature of a function, it is also useful to consider conditions under which a function is strictly concave or strictly convex.

- $f(x)$ is strictly convex if $f''(x) > 0$, except possibly at a single point where $f''(x) = 0$.
- $f(x)$ is strictly concave if $f''(x) < 0$, except possibly at a single point where $f''(x) = 0$.

Example: Consider the function $f(x) = 5x^4$, and determine whether it is strictly concave or convex.

The first and second derivatives are

$$f'(x) = 20x^3,$$
$$f''(x) = 60x^2.$$

It follows that $f(x)$ is strictly convex because $f''(x) > 0$ for all x, except at $x = 0$ where $f''(x) = 0$.

A function is not always strictly concave or convex. In non-strict cases, the graph may contain one or more flat (linear) segments. As shown in Figure 3.4(a), the graph includes a straight-line segment between points A and B. In contrast, the graph of a strictly convex or strictly concave function contains no such linear segments between any two distinct points.

Figure 3.4(b) shows a graph that changes from convex to concave at point P. This point is called an *inflection point.* At an inflection point, the second derivative $f''(x)$ changes sign — for instance, from positive to negative as x increases — and satisfies $f''(x_i) = 0$. The following is a definition of an inflection point.

Definition: If the function $f(x)$ is twice continuously differentiable and $f''(x_i) = 0$, and if the sign of $f''(x)$ changes in the neighborhood of x_i, then the point $(x_i, f(x_i))$ is an inflection point of the function.

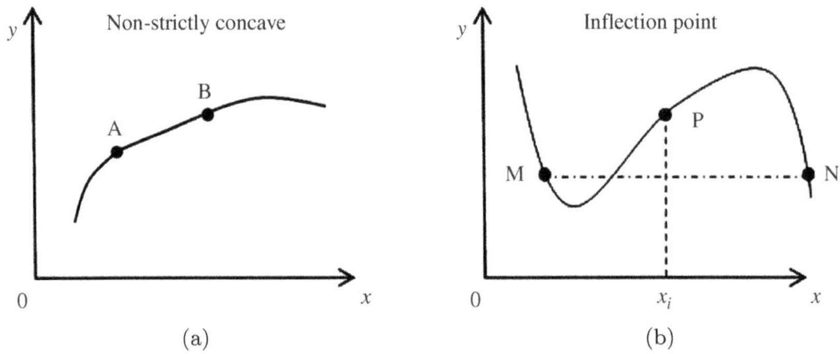

Figure 3.4

It is worth noting that one of the key applications of differential calculus is finding the extreme values of a function. We can identify these values by examining its critical points. For example, consider a function of one variable $y = f(x)$. The first-order condition for a point x_0 to be a critical point is that $f'(x_0) = 0$. To determine whether the critical point is a maximum or minimum, we examine the second derivative. In other words, we can apply the second derivative test to assess whether an extreme value at the critical point is a maximum or minimum, as we will discuss in the next chapter.

3.2.2 *Functions of n variables*

Let $y = f(x_1, x_2)$ be a concave function. The graph of f is shown in Figure 3.5. It depicts two arbitrary points, M and N, on the surface of the function, connected by a line segment. The function is strictly concave if and only if the line segment MN lies entirely below the arc MN, except at M and N.

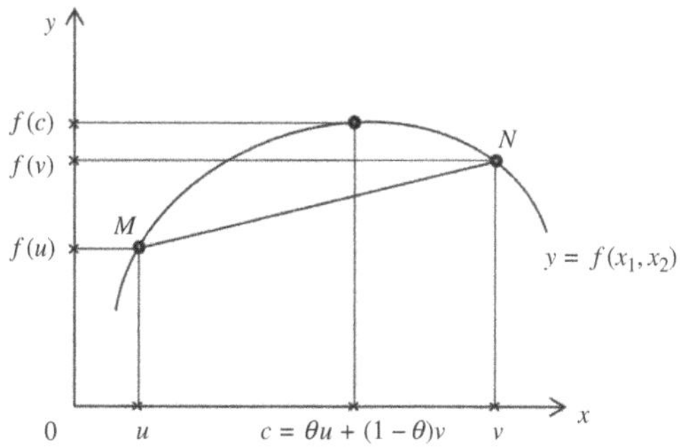

Figure 3.5

Let $u = (u_1, u_2)$ and $v = (v_1, v_2)$ be two distinct ordered pairs in the domain of $f(x_1, x_2)$. The height of the surface corresponding to these pairs is $f(u) = f(u_1, u_2)$ and $f(v) = f(v_1, v_2)$, respectively. We denote the line segment joining u and v as $c = \theta u + (1 - \theta)v$, where θ is a variable in the interval $(0, 1)$. $f(c)$ represents the value of the function f corresponding to any point on the line segment joining u and v. The line segment representing the weighted average of $f(u)$ and $f(v)$ is denoted as $\theta f(u) + (1 - \theta)f(v)$. The following definition summarizes this position regarding the curvature of the function.

Definition: A continuous function f is concave iff, for any pair of distinct points u and v in the convex domain of f, we have

$$f(c) \geq \theta f(u) + (1-\theta)f(v),$$

for all $0 < \theta < 1$, where $c = \theta u + (1-\theta)v$.

A continuous function f is convex iff, for any pair of distinct points u and v in the convex domain of f, we have

$$f(c) \leq \theta f(u) + (1-\theta)f(v),$$

for all $0 < \theta < 1$, where $c = \theta u + (1-\theta)v$.

Note that by replacing the weak inequalities $\leq$ and $\geq$ with strict inequalities $<$ and $>$, the aforementioned definition can be adapted to the case in which the function f is strictly concave or strictly convex. Further, the definition is applicable to a function of n variables.

Example: Consider the function $y = 2x_1^2 + 2x_2^2$, and check whether it is concave or convex.

Let u and v be any two distinct points in the domain of the function. Then, the values of the function at these points are given by

$$f(u) = 2(u_1^2 + u_2^2),$$
$$f(v) = 2(v_1^2 + v_2^2).$$

We denote point c as the weighted average of u and v as follows:

$$c = \theta u + (1-\theta)v, \quad c_1 = \theta u_1 + (1-\theta)v_1, \quad c_2 = \theta u_2 + (1-\theta)v_2,$$

where $0 < \theta < 1$. The value of the function at point c is

$$f(c) = f(\theta u + (1-\theta)v) = 2(\theta u_1 + (1-\theta)v_1)^2 + 2(\theta u_2 + (1-\theta)v_2)^2.$$

The weighted average of $f(u)$ and $f(v)$ is

$$\theta f(u) + (1-\theta)f(v) = 2\theta(u_1^2 + u_2^2) + 2(1-\theta)(v_1^2 + v_2^2).$$

Now, consider the difference

$$\begin{aligned}&\theta f(u) + (1-\theta)f(v) - f(c)\\ &\quad = 2\theta(u_1^2 + u_2^2) + 2(1-\theta)(v_1^2 + v_2^2) - 2(\theta u_1 + (1-\theta)v_1)^2\\ &\quad\quad - 2(\theta u_2 + (1-\theta)v_2)^2.\end{aligned}$$

This simplifies to

$$2\theta(1-\theta)[(u_1 - v_1)^2 + (u_2 - v_2)^2].$$

Since u and v are distinct points, we have $u_1 - v_1 \neq 0$ or $u_2 - v_2 \neq 0$, so the expression in the brackets is positive. Therefore,

$$2\theta(1-\theta)[(u_1 - v_1)^2 + (u_2 - v_2)^2] > 0.$$

It follows that the function $y = 2x_1^2 + 2x_2^2$ is strictly convex, as the difference $\theta f(u) + (1-\theta)f(v) - f(c) > 0$ for all $u \neq v$ and $0 < \theta < 1$.

3.2.3 *Conditions using the Hessian matrix*

The Hessian matrix, $\boldsymbol{H}$, of a function $f(x_1, x_2, \ldots, x_n)$ with n variables is a square matrix with n rows and n columns, whose elements consist of all second-order partial derivatives of f. The Hessian matrix is given by

$$\boldsymbol{H} = \begin{pmatrix} f_{11} & f_{12} & \cdots & f_{1n} \\ f_{21} & f_{22} & \cdots & f_{2n} \\ \vdots & \vdots & \ddots & \vdots \\ f_{n1} & f_{n2} & \cdots & f_{nn} \end{pmatrix},$$

where $f_{ii} = \frac{\partial^2 f}{\partial x_i^2}$ and $f_{ij} = \frac{\partial^2 f}{\partial x_i \partial x_j}$, with $i \neq j$. The principal minors of the Hessian matrix are

$$|\boldsymbol{H}_1| = f_{11},\ |\boldsymbol{H}_2| = \begin{vmatrix} f_{11} & f_{12} \\ f_{21} & f_{22} \end{vmatrix}, \ldots,\ |\boldsymbol{H}_n| = |\boldsymbol{H}|.$$

A function $f(x)$ is concave or convex based on the principal minors of its Hessian matrix. Specifically,

- $f(x)$ is concave if $|\boldsymbol{H}_1| \leq 0,\ |\boldsymbol{H}_2| \geq 0,\ |\boldsymbol{H}_3| \leq 0, \ldots$
- $f(x)$ is convex if $|\boldsymbol{H}_1| \geq 0,\ |\boldsymbol{H}_2| \geq 0,\ |\boldsymbol{H}_3| \geq 0, \ldots$

The conditions for strict concavity and strict convexity can be stated as follows:

- $f(x)$ is strictly concave if $|\boldsymbol{H}_1| < 0,\ |\boldsymbol{H}_2| > 0,\ |\boldsymbol{H}_3| < 0, \ldots$
- $f(x)$ is strictly convex if $|\boldsymbol{H}_1| > 0,\ |\boldsymbol{H}_2| > 0,\ |\boldsymbol{H}_3| > 0, \ldots$

Example: Consider the function $y = 4x_1^2 + 2x_1x_2 + 2x_2^2 + x_1x_3 + 3x_3^2$, and determine its curvature.

The first-order partial derivatives are given by

$$f_1 = 8x_1 + 2x_2 + x_3, \quad f_2 = 2x_1 + 4x_2, \quad f_3 = x_1 + 6x_3.$$

The Hessian matrix of the second-order partial derivatives is

$$\boldsymbol{H} = \begin{pmatrix} 8 & 2 & 1 \\ 2 & 4 & 0 \\ 1 & 0 & 6 \end{pmatrix}.$$

The principal minors of the Hessian matrix are

$$|\boldsymbol{H}_1| = 8,$$

$$|\boldsymbol{H}_2| = 32 - 4 = 28,$$

$$|\boldsymbol{H}_3| = -4 + 168 = 164.$$

Since the principal minors are positive, the function is strictly convex.

3.2.4 *Theorems on concavity and convexity*

Three important theorems characterize whether a function is concave or convex.

Theorem – linear function: If $f(x)$ is a linear function, then it is both concave and convex (but not strictly concave or strictly convex).

Theorem – negative of a function: If $f(x)$ is a concave (convex) function, then $-f(x)$ is convex (concave). Similarly, if $f(x)$ is a strictly concave (strictly convex) function, then $-f(x)$ is strictly convex (strictly concave).

Theorem – sum of functions: If $f(x)$ and $g(x)$ are both concave (convex) functions, then $f(x)+g(x)$ is a concave (convex) function as well. If $f(x)$ and $g(x)$ are both concave (convex) functions, and either one or both of them are strictly concave (strictly convex), then $f(x)+g(x)$ is strictly concave (strictly convex).

Example: Consider the function $y = 2x_1^2 + 2x_2^2$, and using the above-mentioned theorems, check whether it is concave or convex.

To check whether the function is concave or convex, we note that each of the terms $2x_1^2$ and $2x_2^2$ is a strictly convex function as their second derivatives are positive. Since the sum of two strictly convex functions is strictly convex, the function $y = 2x_1^2 + 2x_2^2$ will also be strictly convex.

3.3 Quasi-Concavity and Quasi-Convexity

We examine the conditions under which a function is quasi-concave or quasi-convex. As we will see, every concave (convex) function is also quasi-concave (quasi-convex), but not every quasi-concave (quasi-convex) function is concave (convex). This means that quasi-concavity and quasi-convexity are necessary, but not sufficient, conditions for a function to be concave or convex. For example, Figure 3.6 shows two quasi-concave functions. While some quasi-concave functions are concave, as illustrated by the figure on the left, others may take forms like bell curves or parts of bell curves, and thus are not concave.

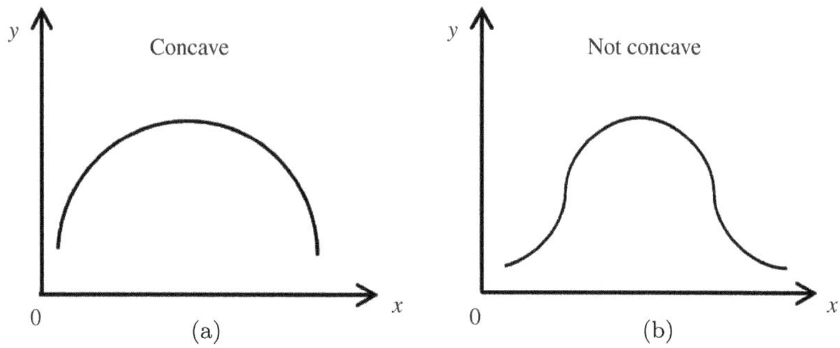

Figure 3.6

From a geometric perspective, Figure 3.7(a) shows a straight line joining two points, M and N, on the curve $y = f(x)$. Suppose that $f(M)$ and $f(N)$ are the values of the function at the points M and N, respectively. A function is quasi-concave if and only if the function value at any point on the line segment joining M and N is at least as large as the minimum of the function values at M and N. This condition ensures that the function does not dip below the minimum value at either of the endpoints along the entire segment.

Definition: A function f is quasi-concave iff, for any pair of distinct points M and N in the convex domain of f, we have

$$f(c) \geq \min\{f(M), f(N)\},$$

for all $0 < \theta < 1$, where $c = \theta M + (1 - \theta)N$.

For strict quasi-concavity, we replace the weak inequality with a strict inequality. That is, the function value at any point on the line segment joining M and N is strictly greater than the minimum of the function values at M and N, except at the points M and N.

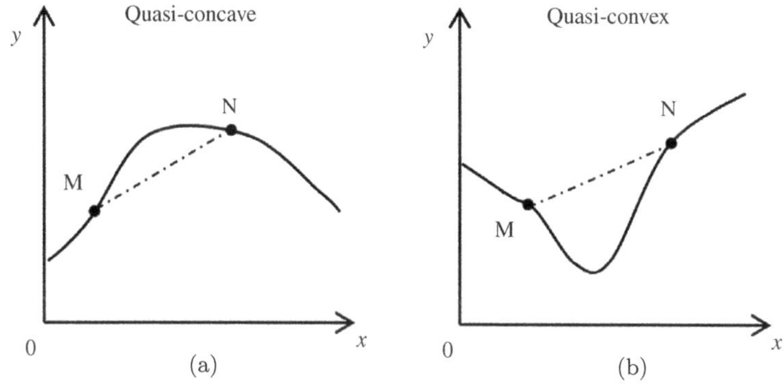

Figure 3.7

Figure 3.7(b) shows that if the function lies below or equal to the line segment joining M and N, the function is quasi-convex. This position is stated more formally in the following definition.

Definition: A function f is quasi-convex iff, for any pair of distinct points M and N in the convex domain of f, we have

$$f(c) \leq \max\{f(M), f(N)\},$$

for all $0 < \theta < 1$, where $c = \theta M + (1 - \theta)N$.

Again, this definition can be adapted to strict quasi-convexity by replacing the weak inequality with a strict inequality. This means that the function value at any point on the line segment joining M and N will be strictly smaller than the maximum of the function values at M and N, except at the points M and N.

3.3.1 *Theorems on quasi-concavity and quasi-convexity*

Similar to the case of concavity and convexity, three important theorems characterize whether a function is quasi-concave or quasi-convex.

Theorem – linear function: If $f(x)$ is a linear function, then it is both quasi-concave and quasi-convex. (However, it is not strictly quasi-concave or strictly quasi-convex, since strict quasi-concavity and quasi-convexity require strict inequality conditions that are not satisfied by linear functions.)

Theorem – negative of a function: If $f(x)$ is a quasi-concave (quasi-convex) function, then $-f(x)$ is quasi-convex (quasi-concave). Similarly, if $f(x)$ is a strictly quasi-concave (strictly quasi-convex) function, then $-f(x)$ is strictly quasi-convex (strictly quasi-concave).

Theorem – concavity (convexity) versus quasi-concavity (quasi-convexity): If $f(x)$ is a concave (convex) function, then $f(x)$ is also quasi-concave (quasi-convex), but the converse does not necessarily hold. Similarly, if $f(x)$ is a strictly concave (strictly convex) function, then $f(x)$ is strictly quasi-concave (strictly quasi-convex), but the converse is not necessarily true either.

3.3.2 *Conditions for quasi-concavity and quasi-convexity*

By constructing the bordered Hessian matrix $\overline{\boldsymbol{H}}$, a modified version of the Hessian matrix, we can determine whether a function is quasi-concave or quasi-convex. The bordered Hessian matrix is given by

$$\overline{\boldsymbol{H}} = \begin{pmatrix} 0 & f_1 & f_2 & \cdots & f_n \\ f_1 & f_{11} & f_{12} & \cdots & f_{1n} \\ f_2 & f_{21} & f_{22} & \cdots & f_{2n} \\ \vdots & \vdots & \vdots & \ddots & \vdots \\ f_n & f_{n1} & f_{n2} & \cdots & f_{nn} \end{pmatrix},$$

where $f_i = \frac{\partial f}{\partial x_i}$ and $f_{ij} = \frac{\partial^2 f}{\partial x_i \partial x_j}$. The principal minors of the bordered Hessian are

$$|\overline{\boldsymbol{H}}_1| = \begin{vmatrix} 0 & f_1 \\ f_1 & f_{11} \end{vmatrix}, \quad |\overline{\boldsymbol{H}}_2| = \begin{vmatrix} 0 & f_1 & f_2 \\ f_1 & f_{11} & f_{12} \\ f_2 & f_{21} & f_{22} \end{vmatrix}, \ldots, |\overline{\boldsymbol{H}}_n| = |\overline{\boldsymbol{H}}|.$$

Using these principal minors, we can express the necessary conditions for quasi-concavity and quasi-convexity for functions defined on the non-negative orthant[2] as follows:

- $f(x)$ is quasi-concave only if $|\overline{\boldsymbol{H}}_1| \leq 0$, $|\overline{\boldsymbol{H}}_2| \geq 0$, $|\overline{\boldsymbol{H}}_3| \leq 0, \ldots$
- $f(x)$ is quasi-convex only if $|\overline{\boldsymbol{H}}_1| \leq 0$, $|\overline{\boldsymbol{H}}_2| \leq 0$, $|\overline{\boldsymbol{H}}_3| \leq 0, \ldots$

Additionally, sufficient conditions for f to be quasi-concave or quasi-convex on the non-negative orthant are

- $f(x)$ is quasi-concave if $|\overline{\boldsymbol{H}}_1| < 0$, $|\overline{\boldsymbol{H}}_2| > 0$, $|\overline{\boldsymbol{H}}_3| < 0, \ldots$
- $f(x)$ is quasi-convex if $|\overline{\boldsymbol{H}}_1| < 0$, $|\overline{\boldsymbol{H}}_2| < 0$, $|\overline{\boldsymbol{H}}_3| < 0, \ldots$

Example: Determine whether the function $f(x_1, x_2) = x_1 x_2$, with x_1, $x_2 > 0$, is quasi-concave or quasi-convex.

We begin by calculating the partial derivatives with respect to x_1 and x_2, which are given by $f_1 = x_2$ and $f_2 = x_1$. Next, we compute the bordered Hessian matrix

$$\overline{\boldsymbol{H}} = \begin{pmatrix} 0 & f_1 & f_2 \\ f_1 & f_{11} & f_{12} \\ f_2 & f_{21} & f_{22} \end{pmatrix} = \begin{pmatrix} 0 & x_2 & x_1 \\ x_2 & 0 & 1 \\ x_1 & 1 & 0 \end{pmatrix}.$$

2 The non-negative orthant in $\mathbb{R}^n$ is the subset of n-dimensional real space in which every coordinate of a vector is non-negative. It can be expressed as $\{x = (x_1, x_2, \ldots, x_n) \in \mathbb{R}^n \mid x_1 \geq 0, x_2 \geq 0, \ldots, x_n \geq 0\}$.

Now, we compute the two principal minors of the bordered Hessian

$$|\overline{\boldsymbol{H}}_1| = -x_2^2,$$

$$|\overline{\boldsymbol{H}}_2| = 2x_1x_2.$$

Given that $|\overline{\boldsymbol{H}}_1| < 0$ and $|\overline{\boldsymbol{H}}_2| > 0$, the function satisfies the sufficient conditions for quasi-concavity. Thus, $f(x_1, x_2) = x_1x_2$ is quasi-concave.

3.4 Further Exercises and Applications

(3.1) Consider the utility function $u(x, y) = x^a + y^b$, where x, $y > 0$. Find the conditions on a and b such that this function is strictly concave.

Solution:

The first-order partial derivatives are $u_x = ax^{a-1}$ and $u_y = by^{b-1}$. The Hessian matrix is given by

$$\boldsymbol{H} = \begin{pmatrix} a(a-1)x^{a-2} & 0 \\ 0 & b(b-1)y^{b-2} \end{pmatrix}.$$

For the utility function to be strictly concave, the signs of the principal minors of the Hessian must alternate, starting with a negative sign: $|\boldsymbol{H}_1| < 0$ and $|\boldsymbol{H}_2| > 0$. The first principal minor is as follows:

$$|\boldsymbol{H}_1| = a(a-1)x^{a-2}.$$

For $|\boldsymbol{H}_1|$ to be negative, we require $a \in (0, 1)$. The second principal minor is as follows:

$$|\boldsymbol{H}_2| = ab(a-1)(b-1)x^{a-2}y^{b-2}.$$

For $|\boldsymbol{H}_2|$ to be positive, we require $b \in (0, 1)$, given that $a \in (0, 1)$. Hence, the utility function will be strictly concave if $a \in (0, 1)$ and $b \in (0, 1)$.

(3.2) Determine whether the function $f(x_1, x_2) = x_1^3 x_2$, with x_1, $x_2 \geq 0$, is quasi-concave or quasi-convex.

Solution:

The first-order partial derivatives are

$$f_1 = 3x_1^2 x_2 \quad \text{and} \quad f_2 = x_1^3.$$

The bordered Hessian matrix is

$$\overline{\boldsymbol{H}} = \begin{pmatrix} 0 & 3x_1^2 x_2 & x_1^3 \\ 3x_1^2 x_2 & 6x_1 x_2 & 3x_1^2 \\ x_1^3 & 3x_1^2 & 0 \end{pmatrix}.$$

The two principal minors are

$$|\overline{\boldsymbol{H}}_1| = -9x_1^4 x_2^2 \leq 0, \quad |\overline{\boldsymbol{H}}_2| = 12x_1^7 x_2 \geq 0.$$

Thus, $f(x)$ is quasi-concave.

(3.3) Consider the profit function $\pi = (100 - q_1 - q_2)(q_1 + q_2) - 2q_1^2 - 3q_2^2$, with q_1, $q_2 > 0$, and confirm that it is strictly concave.

Solution:

We calculate the first-order partial derivatives, which are given by

$$\pi_1 = 100 - 6q_1 - 2q_2 \quad \text{and} \quad \pi_2 = 100 - 2q_1 - 8q_2.$$

The corresponding Hessian matrix is

$$\boldsymbol{H} = \begin{pmatrix} -6 & -2 \\ -2 & -8 \end{pmatrix}.$$

For the profit function to be strictly concave, the signs of the two principal minors of $\boldsymbol{H}$ must alternate, starting with a negative sign:

$$|\boldsymbol{H}_1| = -6 < 0, \quad |\boldsymbol{H}_2| = 44 > 0.$$

Hence, the profit function is strictly concave.

Further Reading

Chiang, A. C. & Wainwright, K. (2005). *Fundamental Methods of Mathematical Economics*. Boston, McGraw-Hill.

Kythe, P. K. (2018). *Elements of Concave Analysis and Applications*. Boca Raton, CRC Press.

Simon, C. P. & Blume, L. (1994). *Mathematics for Economists*. New York, Norton.

Varian, H. R. (1992). *Microeconomics Analysis* (third edition). New York, Norton.

CHAPTER 4

UNCONSTRAINED OPTIMIZATION

Learning Objectives

After completing this chapter, students will be able to:

- Understand the distinction between necessary and sufficient conditions for maximum and minimum points.
- Identify the optimal point of a function with one or more variables.
- Perform a comparative static analysis using the envelope theorem.
- Apply calculus to identify a firm's profit-maximizing output or a consumer's demand for goods.

This chapter is concerned with unconstrained optimization problems, where an objective function is optimized in the absence of any constraint. The chapter presents necessary and sufficient conditions for solving such problems. As we will discuss, the first-order conditions are derived from the partial derivatives of the objective function with respect to each choice variable, and these derivatives are set to zero. The first-order conditions are necessary for optimality and provide candidate points for a local optimum. The next step involves identifying the exact type of each candidate point.

To do this, second-order conditions are employed based on the signs of the principal minors of the Hessian matrix.

4.1 Functions of More Than One Variable

We begin our study of unconstrained optimization problems by considering the concept of a stationary point.[1] The main idea is that, at a stationary point, the slope of the function is equal to zero. This implies that the gradient of the objective function is equal to zero. The following definition summarizes this concept.

Definition: A function $f(x)$ has a stationary point at $x^* = (x_1^*, x_2^*, \ldots, x_n^*)$ if all of its first-order partial derivatives are equal to zero at this point

$$\frac{\partial f}{\partial x_1}(x^*) = 0, \quad \frac{\partial f}{\partial x_2}(x^*) = 0, \ldots, \quad \frac{\partial f}{\partial x_n}(x^*) = 0$$

or

$$\nabla f(x^*) = 0,$$

where $\nabla f(x^*)$ denotes the gradient of $f(x)$ evaluated at x^*. The gradient represents the vector of all first-order partial derivatives of the function with respect to each choice variable at the point x^*.

In many economic applications, a stationary point is a local maximum or minimum. However, the aforementioned definition does not specify which type of stationary point we have.[2] For this reason, an additional condition is required to pinpoint the exact type of the extremum. The following describes this condition.

1 For a more detailed discussion of this topic, see Bergin (2015).

2 Under certain circumstances, we will see that a stationary point can take other forms, such as a saddle point or an inflection point.

Definition: If a function $f(x)$ is defined at some neighborhood of $x^* = (x_1^*, x_2^*, \ldots, x_n^*)$, then $f(x)$ has a local maximum (minimum) at x^* if $f(x^*) - f(x) > 0(< 0)\,\forall x$ in that neighborhood except possibly at x^*.

The intuition is simple: first, choose a neighborhood around the stationary point. If the function attains the highest value at that point compared to any other point in the neighborhood, we say that the stationary point is a local maximum. Similarly, the stationary point is a local minimum if, in a neighborhood around it, the function attains the lowest value at that point. This leads to a two-step approach for solving an unconstrained optimization problem: first, identify the stationary points of the function, and then determine the exact type of each candidate point. The first step corresponds to the first-order necessary condition, while the second step is based on the second-order sufficient condition.

(i) **First-order necessary condition:** If $\frac{\partial f}{\partial x_i}(x^*) = 0\,\forall i = 1, \ldots, n$, then x^* is a candidate point for a local maximum or minimum.

(ii) **Second-order sufficient condition:** The second-order sufficient condition is based on the Hessian matrix $\boldsymbol{H}$, which comprises the second-order partial derivatives of the function. The Hessian at a point x^* is given by

$$\boldsymbol{H}\big|_{x=x^*} = \begin{pmatrix} f_{11} & f_{12} & \cdots & f_{1n} \\ f_{21} & f_{22} & \cdots & f_{2n} \\ & & \cdots & \\ f_{n1} & f_{n2} & \cdots & f_{nn} \end{pmatrix},$$

where $f_{ij} = \frac{\partial^2 f}{\partial x_i \partial x_j}(x^*)$, and $i, j = 1, \ldots, n$.

The Hessian matrix, $\boldsymbol{H}$, is evaluated at each candidate point x^*. To assess whether a candidate point is a local maximum or minimum, we examine the signs of the principal minors of the Hessian matrix, as in Section 3.2.3, where the same conditions were used to determine strict concavity or convexity. Specifically, the following sufficient conditions apply

- x^* is a local maximum if $|\boldsymbol{H}_1| < 0, |\boldsymbol{H}_2| > 0, \ldots$
- x^* is a local minimum if $|\boldsymbol{H}_1| > 0, |\boldsymbol{H}_2| > 0, \ldots$

Example: Consider the function $y = x_1x_2 - 10x_1^2 - 5x_2^2$, and find the values of x_1 and x_2 that optimize this function.

The first-order necessary conditions are

$$\frac{\partial y}{\partial x_1} = x_2 - 20x_1 = 0,$$
$$\frac{\partial y}{\partial x_2} = x_1 - 10x_2 = 0.$$

Solving this system of equations gives us the candidate point (0,0). The second-order sufficient condition is given by the Hessian matrix, which is the matrix of second-order partial derivatives

$$\boldsymbol{H} = \begin{pmatrix} y_{11} & y_{12} \\ y_{21} & y_{22} \end{pmatrix} = \begin{pmatrix} -20 & 1 \\ 1 & -10 \end{pmatrix}.$$

The corresponding principal minors of the Hessian matrix are

$$|\boldsymbol{H}_1| = -20,$$
$$|\boldsymbol{H}_2| = 199.$$

Given that $|\boldsymbol{H}_1| < 0$ and $|\boldsymbol{H}_2| > 0$, we conclude that the point (0,0) is a local maximum. In other words, the value of y is maximized when $x_1 = 0$ and $x_2 = 0$. Furthermore, in addition to being a local maximum, (0,0) is also a global maximum because the function y is strictly concave.

Example: Suppose that a firm produces two products under perfect competition (meaning that the prices of both products are exogenous). The firm's revenue function, $R(q_1, q_2)$, and the cost function, $C(q_1, q_2)$, are given by

$$R = p_1 q_1 + p_2 q_2,$$

$$C = 2q_1^2 + q_1 q_2 + 1.5q_2^2.$$

Thus, the profit function is

$$\pi = R - C = p_1 q_1 + p_2 q_2 - 2q_1^2 - q_1 q_2 - 1.5q_2^2.$$

To find the profit-maximizing quantities, we require that the candidate points q_1^* and q_2^* satisfy the necessary and sufficient conditions. The first-order necessary conditions are

$$\frac{\partial \pi}{\partial q_1} = p_1 - 4q_1 - q_2 = 0,$$

$$\frac{\partial \pi}{\partial q_2} = p_2 - q_1 - 3q_2 = 0.$$

Solving this system of equations yields

$$q_1^* = \frac{3p_1 - p_2}{11}, \quad q_2^* = \frac{4p_2 - p_1}{11}.$$

The second-order sufficient conditions are given by the Hessian matrix

$$\boldsymbol{H} = \begin{pmatrix} \pi_{11} & \pi_{12} \\ \pi_{21} & \pi_{22} \end{pmatrix} = \begin{pmatrix} -4 & -1 \\ -1 & -3 \end{pmatrix}.$$

The principal minors of the Hessian matrix are

$$|\boldsymbol{H}_1| = -4 < 0,$$

$$|\boldsymbol{H}_2| = 11 > 0.$$

Hence, π is strictly concave and (q_1^*, q_2^*) is a global maximum.

We note that it may not always be the case that a negative first principal minor, $|\boldsymbol{H}_1| < 0$, is followed by a positive second principal minor, $|\boldsymbol{H}_2| > 0$. To illustrate, consider the Hessian matrix of a function $y = f(x)$

$$\boldsymbol{H} = \begin{pmatrix} f_{11} & f_{12} & \cdots & f_{1n} \\ f_{21} & f_{22} & \cdots & f_{2n} \\ & & \cdots & \\ f_{n1} & f_{n2} & \cdots & f_{nn} \end{pmatrix}.$$

The discussion up to this point has suggested that if $|\boldsymbol{H}_1| < 0$, $|\boldsymbol{H}_2| > 0, \ldots$, then the candidate point is a local maximum, whereas if $|\boldsymbol{H}_1| > 0$, $|\boldsymbol{H}_2| > 0, \ldots$, the candidate point is a local minimum. Yet, there could also be cases in which these conditions are not satisfied. For example, suppose that the first principal minor is negative, $|\boldsymbol{H}_1| < 0$, and the second principal minor is either zero or negative, $|\boldsymbol{H}_2| = 0$ or $|\boldsymbol{H}_2| < 0$. In this case, it is not possible to determine the exact type of the candidate point based on the conditions presented so far. Nonetheless, if the last principal minor is different from zero, $|\boldsymbol{H}_n(x^*)| \neq 0$, then we say that the function has a saddle point at x^*.

Figure 4.1 depicts a saddle point of the function $y = f(x_1, x_2)$. Notice that the function has a stationary point with respect to both x_1 and x_2, with corresponding value y'. This stationary point is a maximum point in terms of x_1: y' is the highest value of the function when x_1 is varied. However, with respect to x_2, the candidate point is a minimum because y' is the lowest value of the function when x_2 is varied. As a result, this stationary point is both a maximum and a minimum, depending on the direction from which it is examined. We call this a *saddle point.*

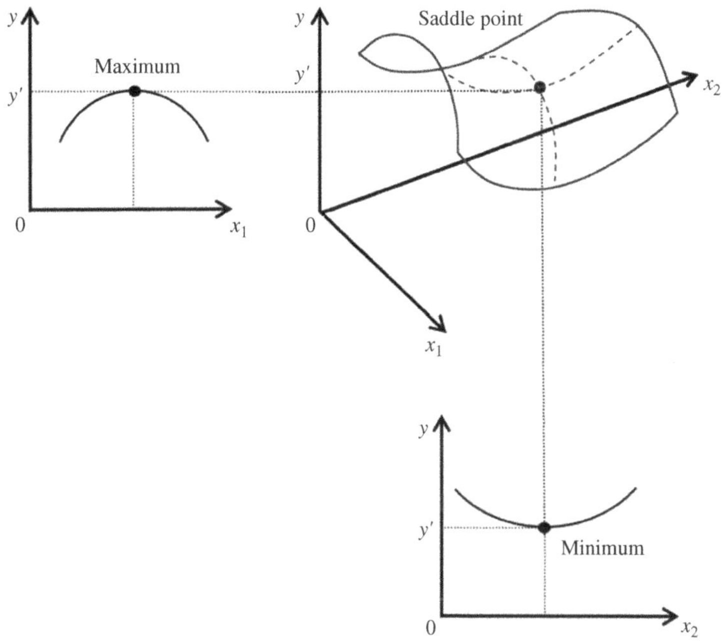

Figure 4.1

4.2 Functions of One Variable

We now consider the case in which a function depends only on one variable, $y = f(x)$. The first-order necessary condition suggests that $x = x_0$ is a stationary point provided that $f'(x_0) = 0$. To pinpoint the exact type of the stationary point, we distinguish between two cases.

- If $f''(x_0) < 0$, then $x = x_0$ is a local maximum.
- If $f''(x_0) > 0$, then $x = x_0$ is a local minimum.

Figure 4.2 depicts a local maximum and a local minimum point. We can see that in the neighborhood of point C, which is a local minimum, the slope of the function tends to increase as x increases.

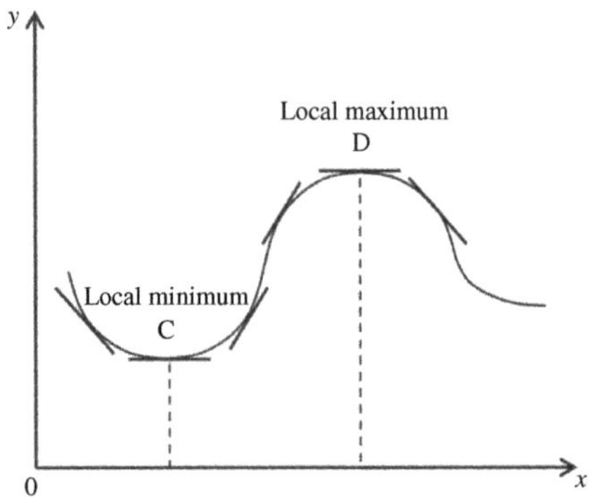

Figure 4.2

Specifically, the slope of the function is initially negative; it becomes zero (at point C); and then turns positive as x increases further. The opposite is true in the neighborhood of point D, which is a local maximum: the slope of the function tends to decrease as x increases; that is, $f''(x_0) < 0$.

Example: Identify the maximum and/or minimum points of the function

$$f(x) = x^3 - 9x^2 + 15x + 11.$$

The first-order necessary condition is

$$f'(x) = 3x^2 - 18x + 15 = 0.$$

Solving the quadratic equation leads to

$$x_1^* = 1 \quad \text{and} \quad x_2^* = 5.$$

The second-order sufficient condition is

$$f''(x) = 6x - 18.$$

Evaluating the second-order condition at each candidate point, we obtain

$$f''(1) = -12 < 0,$$

$$f''(5) = 12 > 0.$$

It follows that the function attains a local maximum at $x_1^* = 1$, and a local minimum at $x_2^* = 5$.

Next, consider the possibility that the second derivative test is not applicable. This may occur if, for instance, the second derivative of a function evaluated at the candidate point is zero, that is, $f''(x_0) = 0$. To shed some light on this issue, consider the function $f(x) = (5 - x)^4$. The first-order condition is

$$f'(x) = -4(5 - x)^3 = 0,$$

which leads to the stationary point $x_0 = 5$. The corresponding second-order condition is

$$f''(x) = 12(5 - x)^2.$$

Evaluating this condition at the candidate point $x_0 = 5$, we obtain

$$f''(5) = 0.$$

This implies that the second derivative test cannot be used here to determine the exact type of the candidate point. Nonetheless, another test is available in this case: the *nth derivative test*, which can be stated as follows.

***n*th derivative test:** If a function $f(x)$ is differentiable n times at $x = x_0$, and all derivatives up to the $(n-1)$th are zero, but the nth derivative is non-zero, i.e., $f^{(n)}(x_0) \neq 0$, then at the stationary point x_0, the function has

(a) a local maximum if n is even and $f^{(n)}(x_0) < 0$;
(b) a local minimum if n is even and $f^{(n)}(x_0) > 0$;
(c) an inflection point if n is odd.

The following example shows how the nth derivative test can be applied.

Example: Consider the function $f(x) = (3 - x)^3$, and determine whether it has a local maximum, local minimum, or inflection point.

We begin by calculating the first derivative

$$f'(x) = -3(3 - x)^2 = 0.$$

Setting $f'(x) = 0$ leads to $x = 3$. Note that

$$f''(x) = 6(3 - x)$$

and evaluating this at $x = 3$ gives

$$f''(3) = 0.$$

Since the second derivative is zero, we continue differentiating the function until we obtain a non-zero derivative at $x = 3$. We find that

$$f^{(3)}(x) = -6.$$

Given that $n = 3$ is odd, we conclude that the point (3, 0) represents an inflection point of the function $f(x) = (3 - x)^3$.

4.3 An Envelope Theorem

We have shown how various unconstrained optimization problems can be solved. The first-order conditions provide candidate points for a local optimum, and second-order conditions are then employed to determine the exact type of each candidate point. After identifying one or more optimal points, we substitute them into the objective function. This yields the value function of the optimization problem. The value function depends on parameters and can be used to conduct a comparative static analysis: by varying one parameter at a time while holding all others constant, we observe how responsive the value function is to that change. This process of examining the sensitivity of the optimal solution is related to an important result known as an envelope theorem.

Theorem: Consider a function $y = f(x, \theta)$, where $x = (x_1, \ldots, x_n)$ is a vector of choice variables and θ is a parameter. The envelope theorem in the context of unconstrained optimization states that the total derivative of the value function V with respect to θ is equal to the partial derivative of the objective function with respect to θ, evaluated at the optimal point. This result can be stated as follows:

$$\frac{dV}{d\theta} = \frac{\partial f(x^*(\theta), \theta)}{\partial \theta}.$$

Example: Consider the profit function $\pi = pf(K, L) - wL - rK$, where p is the price of output, K is capital, L is labor, w is the price per unit of labor, and r is the price per unit of capital. Suppose that the solution to this problem is characterized by the optimal values $K^* = K(w, r, p)$ and $L^* = L(w, r, p)$. Using the envelope theorem, calculate the following partial derivatives: $\partial V/\partial w$, $\partial V/\partial r$ and $\partial V/\partial p$.

The value function of the profit maximization problem is given by

$$\begin{aligned} V(w, r, p) &= \pi^*[K^*(w, r, p), L^*(w, r, p), w, r, p] \\ &= p\,f(K^*, L^*) - wL^* - rK^*. \end{aligned}$$

From the envelope theorem, we obtain

$$\frac{\partial V}{\partial w} = -L^*, \quad \frac{\partial V}{\partial r} = -K^*, \quad \frac{\partial V}{\partial p} = f(K^*, L^*).$$

This result, known as Hotelling's lemma, states that the change in profits due to a change in w is proportional to (the negative of) the demand for labor; the change in profits due to a change in r is proportional to (the negative of) the demand for capital; and the change in profits due to a change in price is proportional to the quantity produced.

4.4 Further Exercises and Applications

(4.1) Consider a monopolist who produces two identical products. The inverse demand function is given by $P = 50 - q_1 - q_2$, where q_1 is the quantity of good 1 and q_2 is the quantity of good 2. The cost functions for goods 1 and 2 are $C_1(q_1) = q_1^2$ and $C_2(q_2) = 2q_2^2$, respectively. Find the profit-maximizing level of output, and determine whether it represents a global maximum.

Solution:

The profit function is given by

$$\pi = (50 - q_1 - q_2)(q_1 + q_2) - q_1^2 - 2q_2^2.$$

The first-order necessary conditions are

$$\pi_1 = 50 - 4q_1 - 2q_2 = 0, \quad \pi_2 = 50 - 2q_1 - 6q_2 = 0.$$

Solving this system of first-order conditions gives the optimal quantities

$$q_1^* = 10, \quad q_2^* = 5.$$

The second-order sufficient conditions involve the Hessian matrix $\boldsymbol{H}$, given by

$$\boldsymbol{H} = \begin{pmatrix} \pi_{11} & \pi_{12} \\ \pi_{21} & \pi_{22} \end{pmatrix} = \begin{pmatrix} -4 & -2 \\ -2 & -6 \end{pmatrix}.$$

The principal minors of the Hessian matrix are

$$|\boldsymbol{H}_1| = -4,$$
$$|\boldsymbol{H}_2| = 20.$$

Given that $|\boldsymbol{H}_1| < 0$ and $|\boldsymbol{H}_2| > 0$, the profit function is strictly concave, implying that the point $(q_1^*, q_2^*) = (10, 5)$ is a global maximum.

(4.2) Consider the utility function $U(x, y) = x^2 + 2y^2$, where $x > 0$ and $y > 0$.

(a) Calculate the first-order partial derivatives, U_x and U_y, and express dU in terms of dx and dy.
(b) Calculate the total derivative dU/dx given the budget line $px + qy = m$, where p is the price of good x, q is the price of good y, and m is income.
(c) Using your answer in part (b), solve for the optimal choices of the goods x and y that maximize utility subject to the budget constraint. There is a problem with your answer. Can you spot it?

Solution:

(a) We find that $U_x = 2x$ and $U_y = 4y$, and thus $dU = 2xdx + 4ydy$.
(b) From part (a), we know that $dU = 2xdx + 4ydy$. Dividing this equation by dx, we obtain

$$\frac{dU}{dx} = 2x + 4y\frac{dy}{dx}.$$

Solving the equation of the budget line for y, we get

$$y = \frac{m}{q} - \frac{p}{q}x,$$

which implies that $dy/dx = -p/q$. Thus

$$\frac{dU}{dx} = 2\left(x - \frac{2p}{q}y\right).$$

(c) To find the optimal choices of x and y, we utilize the following two equations

$$\frac{dU}{dx} = 2\left(x - \frac{2p}{q}y\right) = 0,$$

$$y = \frac{m}{q} - \frac{p}{q}x.$$

Solving the system of the two equations, we obtain the candidate point

$$(x^* y^*) = \left(\frac{2mp}{2p^2 + q^2}, \frac{mq}{2p^2 + q^2}\right).$$

Next, we investigate the curvature of the utility function. The Hessian matrix of the second-order partial derivatives is

$$\boldsymbol{H} = \begin{pmatrix} U_{xx} & U_{xy} \\ U_{yx} & U_{yy} \end{pmatrix} = \begin{pmatrix} 2 & 0 \\ 0 & 4 \end{pmatrix}.$$

The principal minors of the Hessian matrix are

$$|\boldsymbol{H}_1| = 2 > 0,$$

$$|\boldsymbol{H}_2| = 8 > 0.$$

Since the utility function is strictly convex, the solution we found corresponds to a global minimum.

Further Reading

Bergin, J. (2015). *Mathematics for Economists with Applications.* London, Routledge.

Chiang, A. C. & Wainwright, K. (2005). *Fundamental Methods of Mathematical Economics.* Boston, McGraw-Hill.

Silberberg, E. & Suen, W. (2000). *The Structure of Economics: A Mathematical Analysis.* Boston, McGraw-Hill.

Simon, C. P. & Blume, L. (1994). *Mathematics for Economists.* New York, Norton.

Sydsaeter, K., Hammond, P., Seierstad, A. & Strom, A. (2008). *Further Mathematics for Economic Analysis* (second edition). Harlow, Pearson.

Varian, H. R. (1992). *Microeconomics Analysis* (third edition). New York, Norton.

CHAPTER 5

OPTIMIZATION WITH EQUALITY CONSTRAINTS

Learning Objectives

After completing this chapter, students will be able to:

- Use the Lagrange multiplier method to solve optimization problems with equality constraints.
- Understand the interpretation of the Lagrange multiplier.
- Apply the Lagrange multiplier method to various economic problems.

In Chapter 4, we studied how to optimize a function in the absence of constraints. However, economic problems often involve various types of constraints: a consumer may maximize utility subject to a budget constraint or minimize expenditure while attaining a given level of utility. Similarly, a firm may seek to maximize profits or minimize costs under quantity constraints.

This chapter focuses on optimization problems involving equality constraints. We consider cases in which an objective function is optimized subject to one or more binding constraints, meaning they are satisfied with equality. As we will see, such problems are solved using the Lagrange multiplier method. The first-order conditions for constrained optimization are derived by taking the partial derivatives of the Lagrangian function with respect to each choice variable and each Lagrange multiplier, and setting them equal to zero. These conditions yield candidate points for local maxima or minima, much like in the unconstrained case. To determine the exact type of a candidate point, we consider the bordered Hessian matrix and examine the signs of its principal minors.

5.1 Constrained Extreme Points and the Lagrange Multiplier

We start by considering a simple optimization problem. Suppose we wish to find the extreme points, namely the maximum and/or minimum points, of the function $y = f(a, b)$ subject to the constraint

$$g(a, b) = c, \tag{5.1}$$

where c is a constant.

To solve this problem, we define the Lagrangian function as follows:

$$\mathcal{L} = f(a, b) + \lambda[c - g(a, b)]. \tag{5.2}$$

The Lagrangian function is a modified combination of the objective function and the constraint, using a parameter known as the Lagrange multiplier, which is often represented by the Greek letter λ (lambda). We treat the Lagrange multiplier as an additional variable of the Lagrangian function, so $\mathcal{L} = \mathcal{L}(\lambda, a, b)$. If the constraint is satisfied, the last term in the Lagrangian function will vanish, regardless of the value of λ. As a result, the expression for $\mathcal{L}$ becomes identical to the objective function $y = f(a, b)$. This means we no longer need to find the constrained optimum of y.

Instead, we can solve for the unconstrained optimum of $\mathcal{L}$ with respect to a and b.

We now derive the first-order conditions leading to the following set of equations:

$$\mathcal{L}_\lambda \equiv \frac{\partial \mathcal{L}}{\partial \lambda} = 0 \Leftrightarrow c - g(a, b) = 0, \tag{5.3}$$

$$\mathcal{L}_a \equiv \frac{\partial \mathcal{L}}{\partial a} = 0 \Leftrightarrow f_a - \lambda g_a = 0, \tag{5.4}$$

$$\mathcal{L}_b \equiv \frac{\partial \mathcal{L}}{\partial b} = 0 \Leftrightarrow f_b - \lambda g_b = 0. \tag{5.5}$$

We have a system of three equations with three unknowns: a, b, and λ. One way of solving this system is to divide Equation (5.4) by Equation (5.5) in order to eliminate λ. Then, we use the resulting equation along with (5.3) to find the optimal values of a and b, denoted by a^* and b^*. Finally, we substitute a^* and b^* into either (5.4) or (5.5) to obtain the optimal value of λ, denoted λ^*.

Here is an example of how this method can be applied to another constrained optimization problem.

Example: Find the extreme points of the function $f(x, y) = x^{\frac{1}{3}} y^{\frac{2}{3}}$ subject to the constraint $g(x, y) \equiv ax + cy = b$, where a, b and c are constants.

The Lagrangian function is

$$\mathcal{L} = x^{\frac{1}{3}} y^{\frac{2}{3}} + \lambda(b - ax - cy).$$

The first-order conditions are

$$\mathcal{L}_\lambda = b - ax - cy = 0, \tag{5.6}$$

$$\mathcal{L}_x = \frac{1}{3}x^{-\frac{2}{3}}y^{\frac{2}{3}} - \lambda a = 0, \tag{5.7}$$

$$\mathcal{L}_y = \frac{2}{3}x^{\frac{1}{3}}y^{-\frac{1}{3}} - \lambda c = 0. \tag{5.8}$$

Dividing (5.7) by (5.8) leads to

$$y = \frac{2xa}{c}. \tag{5.9}$$

Substituting (5.9) into (5.6) implies

$$x^* = \frac{b}{3a}.$$

Next, inserting the value of x^* into (5.9) gives

$$y^* = \frac{2b}{3c}.$$

Finally, substituting the values for x^* and y^* into either (5.7) or (5.8) leads to

$$\lambda^* = \frac{(y^*)^{\frac{2}{3}}}{3a(x^*)^{\frac{2}{3}}}.$$

Thus, the extreme point is $(\frac{b}{3a}, \frac{2b}{3c})$.

5.2 Second-Order Conditions and the Bordered Hessian Matrix

Suppose we wish to optimize a function of n variables, $y = f(x_1, x_2, \ldots, x_n)$, subject to the constraint $g(x_1, x_2, \ldots, x_n) = b$.

The Lagrangian function for this problem is given by

$$\mathcal{L} = f(x_1, x_2, \ldots, x_n) + \lambda[b - g(x_1, x_2, \ldots, x_n)].$$

The first-order conditions are necessary and provide candidate points for a local maximum or minimum. To determine whether a candidate point is indeed a maximum or minimum, we consider second-order sufficient conditions, which are based on the signs of the principal minors of the bordered Hessian matrix.

We define the bordered Hessian matrix. The first element of this matrix, a_{11}, is zero. The other elements of the first row and the first column consist of the first-order partial derivatives of the constraint with respect to each independent variable, x_i. The remaining elements of the bordered Hessian matrix are the second-order partial derivatives of the Lagrangian function with respect to each choice variable x_i. That is,

$$\overline{\boldsymbol{H}} = \begin{pmatrix} 0 & g_1 & g_2 & \cdots & g_n \\ g_1 & \mathcal{L}_{11} & \mathcal{L}_{12} & \cdots & \mathcal{L}_{1n} \\ g_2 & \mathcal{L}_{21} & \mathcal{L}_{22} & \cdots & \mathcal{L}_{2n} \\ \vdots & \vdots & \vdots & \ddots & \vdots \\ g_n & \mathcal{L}_{n1} & \mathcal{L}_{n1} & \cdots & \mathcal{L}_{nn} \end{pmatrix},$$

where $g_i = \frac{\partial g}{\partial x_i}$, $\mathcal{L}_{ii} = \frac{\partial^2 \mathcal{L}}{\partial x_i^2} = f_{ii} - \lambda g_{ii}$, and $\mathcal{L}_{ij} = \frac{\partial^2 \mathcal{L}}{\partial x_i \partial x_j} = f_{ij} - \lambda g_{ij}$, for $i \neq j$ and $i, j = 1, \ldots, n$. The dimension of the $\overline{\boldsymbol{H}}$ matrix is $(n+1) \times (n+1)$ and its bordered principal minors $|\overline{\boldsymbol{H}}_1|, |\overline{\boldsymbol{H}}_2|, \ldots, |\overline{\boldsymbol{H}}_n| = |\overline{\boldsymbol{H}}|$, are defined as

$$|\overline{\boldsymbol{H}}_1| = \begin{vmatrix} 0 & g_1 \\ g_1 & \mathcal{L}_{11} \end{vmatrix}, \quad |\overline{\boldsymbol{H}}_2| = \begin{vmatrix} 0 & g_1 & g_2 \\ g_1 & \mathcal{L}_{11} & \mathcal{L}_{12} \\ g_2 & \mathcal{L}_{21} & \mathcal{L}_{22} \end{vmatrix}, \ldots$$

with the last principal minor being $|\overline{\boldsymbol{H}}|$ itself. Then, we can state the following sufficient conditions for a local optimum.[1]

(1) The solution to the first-order conditions represents a local minimum if

$$|\overline{\boldsymbol{H}}_2| < 0, |\overline{\boldsymbol{H}}_3| < 0, |\overline{\boldsymbol{H}}_4| < 0, \ldots$$

(2) The solution to the first-order conditions represents a local maximum if

$$|\overline{\boldsymbol{H}}_2| > 0, |\overline{\boldsymbol{H}}_3| < 0, |\overline{\boldsymbol{H}}_4| > 0, \ldots$$

In summary, we can solve a constrained optimization problem using a two-step procedure. First, we derive the first-order conditions by taking the partial derivatives of the Lagrangian function with respect to the choice variables and the Lagrange multiplier, and set them equal to zero. The first-order conditions are necessary and provide candidate points for a local optimum. Second, we identify the type of each candidate point by invoking second-order sufficient conditions and examining the signs of the principal minors of the bordered Hessian matrix.

For a specific example of this two-step procedure, consider the following optimization problem.

Example: Solve for the extreme points of the function $f(w, x) = w^2 + x^2$, subject to the constraint $g(w, x) \equiv 2w + x = -1$.

The Lagrangian function is

$$\mathcal{L} = w^2 + x^2 + \lambda(-1 - 2w - x).$$

1 While these second-order conditions are sufficient, they are not necessary, meaning that a function may have a maximum or minimum without satisfying the conditions. However, for most applications in economics, the second-order sufficient conditions are either satisfied or assumed to be satisfied (Chiang and Wainwright, 2005).

The first-order necessary conditions are

$$\mathcal{L}_\lambda = -1 - 2w - x = 0,$$

$$\mathcal{L}_w = 2w - 2\lambda = 0,$$

$$\mathcal{L}_x = 2x - \lambda = 0.$$

Solving the system of these three equations gives $w^* = -2/5$ and $x^* = -1/5$. The second-order sufficient conditions are given by the bordered Hessian matrix

$$\overline{\boldsymbol{H}} = \begin{pmatrix} 0 & g_w & g_x \\ g_w & \mathcal{L}_{ww} & \mathcal{L}_{wx} \\ g_x & \mathcal{L}_{xw} & \mathcal{L}_{xx} \end{pmatrix} = \begin{pmatrix} 0 & 2 & 1 \\ 2 & 2 & 0 \\ 1 & 0 & 2 \end{pmatrix}.$$

The bordered principal minor is given by

$$|\overline{\boldsymbol{H}}_2|(= |\overline{\boldsymbol{H}}|) = -10 < 0.$$

It follows that the candidate point (w^*, x^*) is a local minimum. Furthermore, it is a global minimum because the condition on the principal minor holds for all values of w and x.

5.3 Multiple Constraints

We consider the case where multiple constraints are present. Suppose there are still n variables and we also have k constraints, with the number of variables exceeding the number of constraints, that is, $n > k$. Our objective is to optimize the function $y = f(x_1, x_2, \ldots, x_n)$ subject to the constraints $g^r(x_1, x_2, \ldots, x_n) = b_r$ for $r = 1, \ldots, k$. Note that in the previous section, we had $r = 1$ (thus r was omitted). The Lagrangian function for this problem is given by

$$\mathcal{L} = f(x_1, x_2, \ldots, x_n) + \sum_{r=1}^{k} \lambda_r [b_r - g^r(x_1, x_2, \ldots, x_n)].$$

The bordered Hessian matrix is defined as

$$\overline{\boldsymbol{H}} = \begin{pmatrix} 0 & \cdots & 0 & g_1^1 & \cdots & g_n^1 \\ \cdots & \cdots & \cdots & \cdots & \cdots & \cdots \\ 0 & \cdots & 0 & g_1^k & \cdots & g_n^k \\ g_1^1 & \cdots & g_1^k & \mathcal{L}_{11} & \cdots & \mathcal{L}_{1n} \\ \cdots & \cdots & \cdots & \cdots & \cdots & \cdots \\ g_n^1 & \cdots & g_n^k & \mathcal{L}_{n1} & \cdots & \mathcal{L}_{nn} \end{pmatrix},$$

where $g_i^r = \partial g^r / \partial x_i$, are the partial derivatives of the constraints with respect to each choice variable x_i, and $\mathcal{L}_{ii}$ and $\mathcal{L}_{ij}$ are the second-order partial derivatives of the Lagrangian function. The $\overline{\boldsymbol{H}}$ matrix is an $(n+k) \times (n+k)$ matrix and its last $(n-k)$ bordered principal minors are

$$|\overline{\boldsymbol{H}}_{k+1}|, |\overline{\boldsymbol{H}}_{k+2}|, \ldots, |\overline{\boldsymbol{H}}_n| (= |\overline{\boldsymbol{H}}|).$$

Consistent with the case of one constraint, $|\overline{\boldsymbol{H}}_1|$ denotes the principal minor whose last element is $\mathcal{L}_{11}$, while $|\overline{\boldsymbol{H}}_2|$ is the principal minor that has $\mathcal{L}_{22}$ as its last element. Using this information, the second-order sufficient conditions for a local maximum or minimum, can be stated as follows.

(1) The solution to the first-order conditions represents a local minimum if all the last $(n-k)$ bordered principal minors have the same sign as $(-1)^k$.

(2) The solution to the first-order conditions represents a local maximum if the last $(n-k)$ bordered principal minors alternate in sign, starting with the sign of $(-1)^{k+1}$.

According to these conditions, we only need to consider $(n-k)$ principal minors to determine the exact type of the critical point. This implies that, for example, if we have three independent variables and two constraints, meaning $n = 3$ and $k = 2$, we check

$n-k=3-2=1$ principal minors, which corresponds to $|\overline{\boldsymbol{H}}|$ itself. Accordingly, if $|\overline{\boldsymbol{H}}|$ takes the sign of $(-1)^2=1>0$, then the critical point will be a local minimum. However, if it takes the sign of $(-1)^3=-1<0$, the critical point will be a local maximum.

5.4 Interpreting the Lagrange Multiplier

The analysis thus far has not provided a specific economic interpretation of the Lagrange multiplier, λ. Instead, λ has been treated as a parameter within the Lagrangian function, enabling the solution of a constrained optimization problem. To clarify the meaning of λ, we consider a simple maximization problem. Our objective is to maximize the utility function

$$U=U(x_1,x_2),$$

subject to the budget constraint $C(x_1,x_2)=m$, which can be expressed as

$$p_1x_1+p_2x_2=m.$$

The Lagrangian function is given by

$$\mathcal{L}=U(x_1,x_2)+\lambda(m-p_1x_1-p_2x_2).$$

The first-order necessary conditions are

$$\mathcal{L}_\lambda=m-p_1x_1-p_2x_2=0,$$

$$\mathcal{L}_{x_1}=U_{x_1}-\lambda p_1=0,$$

$$\mathcal{L}_{x_2}=U_{x_2}-\lambda p_2=0.$$

By dividing the last two equations, we obtain

$$\frac{U_{x_1}}{U_{x_2}}=\frac{p_1}{p_2}.$$

This condition characterizes the optimal solution to the consumer's utility maximization problem. It suggests that, to maximize utility, the consumer equates the ratio of the marginal utilities of the two goods with their price ratio. Rearranging this equation and using $\mathcal{L}_{x_1} = 0$ gives us

$$\frac{U_{x1}}{p_1} = \frac{U_{x2}}{p_2} = \lambda.$$

We observe that the value of good 1 is equal to the value of good 2, and both are equal to λ. In this context, λ represents the marginal utility of income: the effect of relaxing the constraint on the optimal value of the objective function. This interpretation follows from the envelope theorem. If we denote the value of U at the optimum as $V = U(x_1^*, x_2^*)$, where x_1^* and x_2^* are the demands for goods 1 and 2, respectively, then

$$\frac{dV}{dm} = \lambda^*.$$

This relationship illustrates the sensitivity of the optimal value of the utility function to changes in the constraint. For example, if income increases by \$1, assuming all else remains constant, V will increase by an amount equal to λ^*.

We now present an example of how λ can be interpreted in a different context: profit maximization subject to a production constraint.

Example: Suppose the profit function of a firm producing two goods, x_1 and x_2, has the form

$$\Pi(x_1, x_2) = -50 + 40x_1 - 0.05x_1^2 + 50x_2 - 0.1x_2^2.$$

The maximum feasible output is 200 units. The firm's capacity constraint can thus be written as

$$x_1 + x_2 = 200.$$

We seek to find the profit-maximizing quantities x_1^* and x_2^*, along with an interpretation of the Lagrange multiplier.

We begin by writing the Lagrangian function

$$\mathcal{L} = -50 + 40x_1 - 0.05x_1^2 + 50x_2 - 0.1x_2^2 + \lambda(200 - x_1 - x_2).$$

The first-order necessary conditions are

$$\mathcal{L}_{x_1} = 40 - 0.1x_1 - \lambda = 0, \quad (5.10)$$

$$\mathcal{L}_{x_2} = 50 - 0.2x_2 - \lambda = 0, \quad (5.11)$$

$$\mathcal{L}_{\lambda} = 200 - x_1 - x_2 = 0. \quad (5.12)$$

Dividing (5.10) by (5.11) yields

$$x_1 = 2x_2 - 100.$$

Substituting this expression into (5.12) gives $x_2^* = 100$. Next, substituting $x_2^* = 100$ into $x_1 = 2x_2 - 100$ implies $x_1^* = 100$. Using the value of x_1^*, we find from (5.10) that $\lambda^* = 30$.

The second-order sufficient conditions can be assessed using the bordered Hessian matrix, which is given by

$$\overline{\boldsymbol{H}} = \begin{pmatrix} 0 & 1 & 1 \\ 1 & -0.1 & 0 \\ 1 & 0 & -0.2 \end{pmatrix}.$$

The bordered principal minor is

$$|\overline{\boldsymbol{H}}| = 0.3.$$

Given that $|\overline{\boldsymbol{H}}| > 0$ for all values of x_1 and x_2, the candidate point (x_1^*, x_2^*) is a global maximum of the profit-maximization problem. Note further that the firm's profit at the optimal output level is $\Pi^*(100, 100) = \$7450$. Given $\lambda^* = 30$, if the capacity constraint changes by just 1 unit, the firm's profit at the optimum (or maximum profit) will change by \$30.

5.5 Further Exercises and Applications

(5.1) Find the extreme points of the function $f(u, v) = uv$, subject to the constraint $g(u, v) \equiv u + v = 12$.

Solution:

The Lagrangian function is given by

$$\mathcal{L} = uv + \lambda(12 - u - v).$$

The first-order necessary conditions are

$$\mathcal{L}_\lambda = 12 - u - v = 0, \tag{5.13}$$

$$\mathcal{L}_u = v - \lambda = 0, \tag{5.14}$$

$$\mathcal{L}_v = u - \lambda = 0. \tag{5.15}$$

Dividing (5.14) by (5.15) yields

$$u = v.$$

Substitution of $u = v$ into (5.13) gives $u^* = v^* = 6$. Then, substituting these values into either (5.14) or (5.15) provides $\lambda^* = 6$.

The second-order sufficient condition is determined by the bordered Hessian matrix

$$\overline{\boldsymbol{H}} = \begin{pmatrix} 0 & 1 & 1 \\ 1 & 0 & 1 \\ 1 & 1 & 0 \end{pmatrix}.$$

The corresponding principal minor of this matrix is

$$|\overline{\boldsymbol{H}}| = 2 > 0.$$

Thus, the candidate point (u^*, v^*) is a local maximum of the optimization problem. This point is also a global maximum because the condition on the principal minor holds for all values of u and v.

(5.2) A firm has the Cobb–Douglas production function $Q = L^{0.2}K^{0.8}$, where L is labor and K is capital. Suppose the firm can only afford a maximum of \$200 worth of labor and capital, whose prices are $w = 3$ and $r = 15$, respectively. The firm thus faces the constraint $C(L, K) \equiv 3L + 15K = 200$.

(a) What are the optimal values of capital and labor that maximize the firm's output?
(b) Do the optimal values of capital and labor identified in part (a) constitute a global maximum?
(c) What is the maximum output given the constraint?
(d) How much would the output change if the firm could allocate \$100 more on combined labor and capital spending?
(e) What is the maximum level of production with no constraint?

Solution:

(a) The Lagrangian function is given by

$$\mathcal{L} = L^{0.2}K^{0.8} + \lambda(200 - 3L - 15K).$$

The first-order conditions are

$$\mathcal{L}_L = 0.2L^{-0.8}K^{0.8} - 3\lambda = 0, \tag{5.16}$$

$$\mathcal{L}_K - 0.8L^{0.2}K^{-0.2} - 15\lambda = 0, \tag{5.17}$$

$$\mathcal{L}_\lambda = 200 - 3L - 15K = 0. \tag{5.18}$$

Dividing (5.16) by (5.17) yields

$$K = 0.8L.$$

Substituting $K = 0.8L$ into (5.18), and solving for L gives

$$L^* \approx 13.33.$$

Then substituting L^* into (5.18), and solving for K gives

$$K^* \approx 10.66.$$

(b) The second-order sufficient condition is based on the bordered Hessian matrix

$$\overline{\boldsymbol{H}} = \begin{pmatrix} 0 & C_L & C_K \\ C_L & \mathcal{L}_{LL} & \mathcal{L}_{LK} \\ C_K & \mathcal{L}_{KL} & \mathcal{L}_{KK} \end{pmatrix}$$

$$= \begin{pmatrix} 0 & 3 & 15 \\ 3 & -0.16L^{-1.8}K^{0.8} & 0.16L^{-0.8}K^{-0.2} \\ 15 & 0.16L^{-0.8}K^{-0.2} & -0.16L^{0.2}K^{-1.2} \end{pmatrix}.$$

The principal minor of this matrix is

$$|\overline{\boldsymbol{H}}| = 1.44L^{0.2}K^{-1.2} + 14.4L^{-0.8}K^{-0.2} + 36L^{-1.8}K^{0.8} > 0.$$

Thus, it follows that (K^*, L^*) is a global maximum.

(c) The maximum value of the firm's output is found by substituting the optimal values of capital and labor into the objective function, which leads to

$$Q^* \approx 11.15.$$

(d) Substituting K^* and L^* into (5.16) gives $\lambda^* \approx 0.0558$, which reflects the extent to which the maximum value of the objective function changes if we relax the constraint. This implies that if the firm can allocate \$100 more for combined labor and capital spending, its output will increase by approximately 5.58 units.

(e) In the absence of any constraint, there will be no limit on the level of production: $K^{0.8}$ would increase indefinitely as K increases, and so would $L^{0.2}$ as L increases. This scenario violates the fundamental economic principle of scarcity, thereby rendering the maximization problem economically meaningless.

Further Reading

Chiang, A. C. & Wainwright, K. (2005). *Fundamental Methods of Mathematical Economics.* Boston, McGraw-Hill.

Silberberg, E. & Suen, W. (2000). *The Structure of Economics: A Mathematical Analysis.* Boston, McGraw-Hill.

Simon, C. P. & Blume, L. (1994). *Mathematics for Economists.* New York, Norton.

Sydsaeter, K., Hammond, P., Seierstad, A. & Strom, A. (2008). *Further Mathematics for Economic Analysis* (second edition). Harlow, Pearson.

Varian, H. R. (1992). *Microeconomics Analysis* (third edition). New York, Norton.

CHAPTER 6

OPTIMIZATION WITH INEQUALITY CONSTRAINTS

Learning Objectives

After completing this chapter, students will be able to:

- Understand how methods of solving constrained optimization problems can be extended to include inequality constraints.
- Apply the Kuhn–Tucker conditions to solve optimization problems with inequality constraints.
- Recognize the circumstances under which the Kuhn–Tucker conditions are necessary and sufficient.

Chapter 5 focused on optimization problems with equality constraints. Our main objective was to identify the extreme points of a function subject to one or more binding constraints. The current chapter extends these methods to address the more general case of inequality constraints. For example, a consumer may wish to spend some, but not all, of her budget, while a firm might utilize only a portion of its available resources. In both cases, the constraint functions are not satisfied as equalities.

In the case of equality constraints, we established that the first-order conditions correspond to the first-order partial derivatives of the Lagrangian function with respect to the choice variables and the Lagrange multiplier, all of which are set equal to zero. Similar conditions apply in the case of inequality constraints and are known as the Kuhn–Tucker conditions.[1] However, while the first-order conditions in optimization problems with equality constraints are necessary for a solution, the same cannot be said for the Kuhn–Tucker conditions. As we will see, these conditions must satisfy specific requirements to qualify as necessary conditions. Additionally, we will explore the circumstances under which the Kuhn–Tucker conditions are not only necessary but also sufficient.

6.1 The Kuhn–Tucker Conditions

To fix ideas, consider a simple profit maximization problem

$$\max_{q} \pi = f(q)$$
$$\text{subject to } q \geq 0,$$

where f is assumed to be differentiable. Given the restriction on the firm's output, $q \geq 0$, the possible solutions correspond to different points within the feasible region. Figures 6.1(a)–6.1(c) illustrate these solutions.

The first possibility, shown in Figure 6.1(a), suggests that the solution is attained at point A. At this stationary point, we have $df(q)/dq = f'(q) = 0$. Additionally, at point A, the choice variable is positive and the corresponding value of the function is at its maximum.[2] A second possibility is illustrated in Figure 6.1(b), where point B represents the maximum. Here, the first-order condition still holds, $f'(q) = 0$, but the choice variable is equal to zero.

1 This idea originates in Kuhn and Tucker's (1951) seminal contribution.
2 Note that the second-order sufficient condition is $f''(q) < 0$.

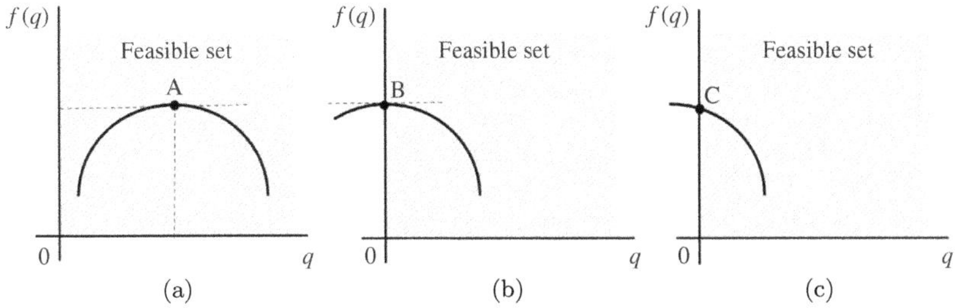

Figure 6.1

The third possibility is shown in Figure 6.1(c), where at point C, the first-order condition is negative, $f'(q) < 0$. In fact, the second and third cases imply a boundary solution: the constraint on the variable is binding (i.e., $q = 0$), and the maximum is attained at the boundary of the feasible set.

Combining the conditions from the three possible cases, we can express them as

$$f'(q) \leq 0, \quad q \geq 0.$$

The second inequality represents a non-negativity restriction on the choice variable, which reflects the requirement that the firm's output must be non-negative. At the optimum, either $q = 0$ or $f'(q) = 0$. We can summarize this as

$$qf'(q) = 0.$$

This equation indicates that at least one of the two terms in the product must be zero, and it is known as the complementary slackness condition between q and $f'(q)$. Generalizing to n choice variables, we can write

$$f_j \leq 0, \quad x_j \geq 0, \quad x_j f_j = 0$$

where $f_j = \partial f / \partial x_j$ for $j = 1, 2, \ldots, n$. This set of conditions constitutes the Kuhn–Tucker conditions in a problem where the choice variables must be non-negative.

Next, we consider a maximization problem with two choice variables and one constraint

$$\max_{q_1,q_2} \pi = f(q_1, q_2)$$
$$\text{subject to } g(q_1, q_2) \leq r$$
$$\text{and } q_1, q_2 \geq 0.$$

The Lagrangian function of this problem is

$$\mathcal{L} = f(q_1, q_2) + \lambda[r - g(q_1, q_2)].$$

The Kuhn–Tucker conditions are

$$\frac{\partial \mathcal{L}}{\partial q_1} \leq 0, \quad q_1 \geq 0, \quad q_1 \frac{\partial \mathcal{L}}{\partial q_1} = 0$$
$$\frac{\partial \mathcal{L}}{\partial q_2} \leq 0, \quad q_2 \geq 0, \quad q_2 \frac{\partial \mathcal{L}}{\partial q_2} = 0$$
$$\frac{\partial \mathcal{L}}{\partial \lambda} \geq 0, \quad \lambda \geq 0, \quad \lambda \frac{\partial \mathcal{L}}{\partial \lambda} = 0.$$

The first inequalities in the first and second sets of conditions correspond to the first-order partial derivative of the Lagrangian with respect to the choice variables. The first inequality in the third set of conditions essentially reinstates the constraint of the problem. Additionally, the second inequalities in all three sets represent the non-negativity restrictions on the choice variables and the Lagrange multiplier. Finally, the third equalities are the complementary slackness conditions. The first two, $q_1(\partial\mathcal{L}/\partial q_1) = 0$ and $q_2(\partial\mathcal{L}/\partial q_2) = 0$, imply that either the choice variable or the corresponding first-order condition is zero. Similarly, $\lambda\frac{\partial \mathcal{L}}{\partial \lambda} = 0$ indicates that either the Lagrange multiplier is zero or the constraint is binding.

More generally, for a maximization problem of n choice variables ($j = 1, 2, \ldots, n$) and k constraints ($i = 1, 2, \ldots, k$), the Kuhn–Tucker conditions can be stated as follows:

$$\frac{\partial \mathcal{L}}{\partial x_j} \leq 0, \quad x_j \geq 0, \quad x_j \frac{\partial \mathcal{L}}{\partial x_j} = 0,$$

$$\frac{\partial \mathcal{L}}{\partial \lambda_i} \geq 0, \quad \lambda_i \geq 0, \quad \lambda_i \frac{\partial \mathcal{L}}{\partial \lambda_i} = 0.$$

These conditions include the first-order conditions for the choice variables and the constraints, along with the non-negativity restrictions and the complementary slackness conditions.

Example: Consider the following problem where an individual maximizes her utility U as a function of goods x and y, subject to a budget constraint and a ration constraint on the amount of good x.

$$\max_{x,y} U = xy$$

$$\text{subject to } x + y \leq 300$$

$$x \leq 100$$

$$\text{and } x, y \geq 0.$$

This is a maximization problem with inequality constraints. The Lagrangian function is

$$\mathcal{L} = xy + \lambda_1(300 - x - y) + \lambda_2(100 - x).$$

The Kuhn–Tucker conditions are

$$\begin{aligned}
&\mathcal{L}_x = y - \lambda_1 - \lambda_2 \leq 0, && x \geq 0, && x\mathcal{L}_x = 0 \\
&\mathcal{L}_y = x - \lambda_1 \leq 0, && y \geq 0, && y\mathcal{L}_y = 0 \\
&\mathcal{L}_{\lambda_1} = 300 - x - y \geq 0, && \lambda_1 \geq 0, && \lambda_1\mathcal{L}_{\lambda_1} = 0 \\
&\mathcal{L}_{\lambda_2} = 100 - x \geq 0, && \lambda_2 \geq 0, && \lambda_2\mathcal{L}_{\lambda_2} = 0.
\end{aligned}$$

It is worth noting that if we have a minimization problem, we can transform it into a maximization problem by multiplying the objective function by −1. We must also multiply the constraint functions by −1 so that they conform to the standard form of constraints in a maximization problem. Alternatively, one can state directly the Kuhn–Tucker conditions for a minimization problem of n choice variables ($j = 1, 2, \ldots, n$) and k constraints ($i = 1, 2, \ldots, k$) as follows:

$$\frac{\partial \mathcal{L}}{\partial x_j} \geq 0, \quad x_j \geq 0, \quad x_j \frac{\partial \mathcal{L}}{\partial x_j} = 0,$$

$$\frac{\partial \mathcal{L}}{\partial \lambda_i} \leq 0, \quad \lambda_i \geq 0, \quad \lambda_i \frac{\partial \mathcal{L}}{\partial \lambda_i} = 0.$$

In comparison to a maximization problem, notice that the inequality signs of the partial derivatives of the Lagrangian with respect to the choice variables x_j and the Lagrange multipliers λ_i are reversed.

Example: Transform the following minimization problem into an equivalent maximization problem, and state the Lagrangian function and the Kuhn–Tucker conditions.

$$\min_{x_1, x_2} f(x_1, x_2) = 2x_1^2 + x_2^2$$

$$\text{subject to } x_1 + x_2 \geq 20$$

$$\text{and } x_1, x_2 \geq 0.$$

Let $h(x_1, x_2)$ be the transformed objective function to be maximized. By multiplying both the objective function and the constraint by −1, we obtain

$$\max_{x_1, x_2} h(x_1, x_2) = -2x_1^2 - x_2^2$$

$$\text{subject to } -x_1 - x_2 \leq -20$$

$$\text{and } x_1, x_2 \geq 0.$$

The Lagrangian function is

$$\mathcal{L} = -2x_1^2 - x_2^2 + \lambda(-20 + x_1 + x_2).$$

And the Kuhn–Tucker conditions are

$$\begin{aligned}
&\mathcal{L}_1 = -4x_1 + \lambda \leq 0, && x_1 \geq 0, && x_1\mathcal{L}_1 = 0,\\
&\mathcal{L}_2 = -2x_2 + \lambda \leq 0, && x_2 \geq 0, && x_2\mathcal{L}_2 = 0,\\
&\mathcal{L}_\lambda = -20 + x_1 + x_2 \geq 0, && \lambda \geq 0, && \lambda\mathcal{L}_\lambda = 0.
\end{aligned}$$

6.2 Solving the Optimization Problem

One common way to solve optimization problems with inequality constraints is through trial and error. As an example, let us return to the utility maximization problem discussed earlier.

$$\max_{x,y} U = xy$$
$$\text{subject to } x + y \leq 300$$
$$x \leq 100$$
$$\text{and } x, y \geq 0.$$

The Lagrangian is

$$\mathcal{L} = xy + \lambda_1(300 - x - y) + \lambda_2(100 - x).$$

The Kuhn–Tucker conditions are

$$\begin{aligned}
&\mathcal{L}_x = y - \lambda_1 - \lambda_2 \leq 0, && x \geq 0, && x(y - \lambda_1 - \lambda_2) = 0,\\
&\mathcal{L}_y = x - \lambda_1 \leq 0, && y \geq 0, && y(x - \lambda_1) = 0,\\
&\mathcal{L}_{\lambda_1} = 300 - x - y \geq 0, && \lambda_1 \geq 0, && \lambda_1(300 - x - y) = 0,\\
&\mathcal{L}_{\lambda_2} = 100 - x \geq 0, && \lambda_2 \geq 0, && \lambda_2(100 - x) = 0.
\end{aligned}$$

We start our search for a solution from the complementary slackness conditions. The first two conditions imply that either a choice variable is zero or the first-order partial derivative of the Lagrangian with respect to that variable is zero. Likewise, the last two conditions suggest that either the Lagrange multiplier is zero or a constraint is binding. We follow through the implications of each case and use the other equations. This procedure provides a *trial solution*, which is acceptable as a final solution if it does not violate the Kuhn–Tucker conditions.

Suppose first that both choice variables, x and y, are positive. This seems reasonable here, given that we are maximizing utility and x and y represent the amounts of the two goods. Notice that if either x or y were zero, then U would also be zero. By complementary slackness, we have $\mathcal{L}_x = y - \lambda_1 - \lambda_2 = 0$ and $\mathcal{L}_y = x - \lambda_1 = 0$. Thus, we can write

$$x = \lambda_1 > 0, \tag{6.1}$$

$$y - \lambda_2 = x. \tag{6.2}$$

Given that $\lambda_1 > 0$, it must be that the budget constraint is binding. Assume that the rationing constraint is not binding, which implies that $\lambda_2 = 0$. Substituting into (6.2) gives $x = y$. From (6.1), we find $x = y = \lambda_1$. Since $x + y = 300$ and $x = y$, we get

$$x = 150 = y.$$

However, these values violate the rationing constraint $x \leq 100$. Therefore, it must be the case that $\lambda_2 > 0$, indicating that the rationing constraint is binding. This leads to $x = 100$. We can then obtain the other solution values: from (6.1), $\lambda_1 = 100$; from the budget constraint, $y = 200$; and from (6.2), $\lambda_2 = 100$. It is straightforward to verify that these values satisfy the Kuhn–Tucker conditions. Thus, these values constitute the solution to the utility maximization problem.

Example: Consider the following minimization problem

$$\min_{a,b} C = (a-8)^2 + (b-8)^2$$

$$\text{subject to } 2a + 3b \geq 10$$

$$-3a - 2b \geq -20$$

$$\text{and } a, b \geq 0.$$

The Lagrangian function is

$$\mathcal{L} = (a-8)^2 + (b-8)^2 + \lambda_1(10 - 2a - 3b) + \lambda_2(-20 + 3a + 2b).$$

Since we have a minimization problem, the Kuhn–Tucker conditions are

$$\begin{aligned}
&\mathcal{L}_a = 2(a-8) - 2\lambda_1 + 3\lambda_2 \geq 0, && a \geq 0, && a[2(a-8) - 2\lambda_1 + 3\lambda_2] = 0,\\
&\mathcal{L}_b = 2(b-8) - 3\lambda_1 + 2\lambda_2 \geq 0, && b \geq 0, && b[2(b-8) - 3\lambda_1 + 2\lambda_2] = 0,\\
&\mathcal{L}_{\lambda_1} = 10 - 2a - 3b \leq 0, && \lambda_1 \geq 0, && \lambda_1(10 - 2a - 3b) = 0,\\
&\mathcal{L}_{\lambda_2} = -20 + 3a + 2b \leq 0, && \lambda_2 \geq 0, && \lambda_2(-20 + 3a + 2b) = 0.
\end{aligned}$$

Suppose first that both constraints are binding, which implies that $\lambda_1 > 0$ and $\lambda_2 > 0$. Thus, we have $2a + 3b = 10$ and $3a + 2b = 20$. Solving the system of these two equations in two unknowns yields $a = 8$ and $b = -2$. However, this solution violates the non-negativity restriction $b \geq 0$. Hence, it must be that either λ_1 or λ_2, or both, are zero, implying three possible cases: (i) $\lambda_1 = 0$ and $\lambda_2 > 0$; (ii) $\lambda_1 > 0$ and $\lambda_2 = 0$; and (iii) $\lambda_1 = 0$ and $\lambda_2 = 0$. Assuming that $a, b > 0$, we can write

$$2(a-8) - 2\lambda_1 + 3\lambda_2 = 0, \tag{6.3}$$

$$2(b-8) - 3\lambda_1 + 2\lambda_2 = 0. \tag{6.4}$$

Multiplying (6.3) by 2 and (6.4) by 3 gives

$$4(a-8) - 4\lambda_1 + 6\lambda_2 = 0, \tag{6.3$'$}$$

$$6(b-8) - 9\lambda_1 + 6\lambda_2 = 0. \tag{6.4$'$}$$

Subtracting (6.4′) from (6.3′) yields

$$4a - 6b + 16 + 5\lambda_1 = 0. \tag{6.5}$$

Now, suppose that the first case of the restrictions on λ_1 and λ_2 is valid, namely $\lambda_1 = 0$ and $\lambda_2 > 0$. Then (6.5) becomes

$$2a - 3b = -8. \tag{6.6}$$

Moreover, $\lambda_2 > 0$ implies

$$3a + 2b = 20. \tag{6.7}$$

Solving the system of (6.6) and (6.7) gives

$$a = \frac{44}{13}, \quad b = \frac{64}{13}.$$

Substituting the value of a into (6.3) or the value of b into (6.4) yields $\lambda_2 = 40/13 > 0$. Thus, we have the following set of trial solution values: $a = 44/13$, $b = 64/13$, $\lambda_1 = 0$ and $\lambda_2 = 40/13$. These solution values satisfy the Kuhn–Tucker conditions, allowing us to accept them as the solution to the minimization problem.

6.3 Necessity of the Kuhn–Tucker Conditions

We have learned that the techniques for solving optimization problems with inequality constraints are based on the Kuhn–Tucker conditions. We also established in the previous chapter that the first-order conditions for optimization problems with equality constraints are necessary for identifying local maximum or minimum points. This raises a natural question: Are the Kuhn–Tucker conditions necessary conditions?

The Kuhn–Tucker conditions are necessary only if a specific requirement, known as the *constraint qualification*, is satisfied. The constraint qualification is a regularity condition that imposes certain restrictions on the constraints, ensuring that the optimal solution of the problem adheres to the Kuhn–Tucker conditions. In other words, as long as the constraint qualification holds, the solution of the optimization problem coincides with the solution identified by the Kuhn–Tucker conditions. It is important to note that when the constraint functions are linear, the constraint qualification is always satisfied. However, constraint functions can also be nonlinear. In such cases, Arrow and Enthoven proposed a test to determine whether the constraint qualification holds.[3]

A constraint-qualification test: Consider the following maximization problem

$$\max_{x} f(x)$$

$$\text{subject to } g^i(x) \leq c_i \quad (i = 1, \ldots, k)$$

$$\text{and } x \geq 0.$$

If the following conditions hold:

(a) Every constraint function $g^i(x)$ is differentiable and quasi-convex.
(b) There exists a point x_0 in the non-negative orthant, such that all the constraints are satisfied as strict inequalities at x_0.
(c) At least one of the following is true:

(c–i) Every $g^i(x)$ function is convex.
(c–ii) The partial derivatives of each $g^i(x)$ are not all zero when evaluated at every point x in the feasible region.

Then, the constraint qualification is satisfied.

[3] The reader can also consult Arrow and Enthoven (1961) and Chiang and Wainwright (2005).

Although this test deals with a maximization problem, it can be easily adapted to a minimization problem. To do this, we first rewrite the problem as a minimization problem. Then, in condition (a), we replace the term "quasi-convex" with "quasi-concave", and in condition (c–i), we change "convex" to "concave". Here is an example illustrating how the Arrow and Enthoven constraint qualification test can be applied.

Example: Consider the constraints $x^2 + y^2 \leq 1$ and $x - 2y \leq 0$ in a given maximization problem. Are the Kuhn–Tucker conditions necessary for a solution?

Let $g^1(x, y) = x^2 + y^2$ and $g^2(x, y) = x - 2y$. The constraint function g^1 is nonlinear, so we apply Arrow and Enthoven's constraint qualification test. First, both constraint functions g^1 and g^2 are differentiable. In addition, g^1 is a convex function and therefore quasi-convex; g^2 is also a quasi-convex function since it is linear (and hence convex). Second, there exists a point in the non-negative orthant, such as $(1/3,\ 1/3)$, that satisfies the constraints as strict inequalities. Third, both g^1 and g^2 are convex functions. It follows that the constraint qualification is satisfied, and therefore the Kuhn–Tucker conditions are necessary conditions for a maximum.

6.4 Sufficiency of the Kuhn–Tucker Conditions

We now consider the circumstances under which the Kuhn–Tucker conditions are sufficient for a solution. In classical optimization problems — whether without constraints or with equality constraints — the second-order conditions help determine whether a candidate point is indeed a local maximum or minimum. As we discussed in Chapters 4 and 5, these conditions closely reflect the concepts of concavity and convexity of the objective function. The same is also true for optimization problems with inequality constraints. More specifically, Kuhn and Tucker developed sufficient conditions regarding both the objective function and the constraint functions for such problems.[4]

Sufficiency theorem: If the following conditions are satisfied

(a) The objective function $f(x)$ is differentiable and concave in the non-negative orthant.
(b) Each constraint function $g^i(x)$ is differentiable and convex in the non-negative orthant.
(c) A point x^* satisfies the Kuhn–Tucker conditions.

Then, the point x^* is a global maximum of $f(x)$.

This theorem can be easily adapted to the case of a minimization problem by simply interchanging the terms "concave" and "convex" in conditions (a) and (b). Note also that the theorem does not explicitly mention the constraint qualification because the Kuhn–Tucker conditions are satisfied by condition (c). Furthermore, we know that the Kuhn–Tucker conditions are necessary only if the constraint qualification holds, which is always true for linear constraint functions. Combining this result with the aforementioned Kuhn–Tucker sufficiency theorem, we can conclude that if conditions (a) and (b) of the theorem are satisfied and the constraint qualification holds, then the Kuhn–Tucker conditions are both necessary and sufficient conditions for a solution.

---

4 Another sufficiency theorem presents weaker sufficient conditions (see Arrow and Enthoven, 1961). This theorem relaxes the requirement for concavity in the objective function and convexity in the constraints to quasi-concavity and quasi-convexity, respectively, thereby making it easier to satisfy the sufficient conditions.

Example: Consider the problem

$$\min_{x_1,x_2} f(x_1,x_2) = x_1^2 + 2x_2^2$$

$$\text{subject to } x_1 + x_2 \geq 20$$

$$\text{and} \quad x_1, x_2 \geq 0.$$

Are the Kuhn–Tucker conditions necessary and sufficient for a solution to this problem?

The objective function is convex (see Exercise 4.2), and the constraint functions are linear. The convexity of the objective function implies that condition (a) of the Kuhn–Tucker sufficiency theorem is satisfied, while the linearity of the constraints means that both condition (b) of the theorem and the constraint qualification hold. Therefore, the Kuhn–Tucker conditions are both necessary and sufficient: the solution to the problem coincides with the solution identified by the Kuhn–Tucker conditions.

6.5 Further Exercises and Applications

(6.1) Consider the problem

$$\min_{x} C = 2(x-2)^2$$

$$\text{subject to } x \geq \tfrac{3}{2}.$$

Find the solution to this problem using the Kuhn–Tucker Conditions.

Solution:

The objective function is convex and the constraint is linear. Thus, the Kuhn–Tucker conditions are both necessary and sufficient for a solution to the minimization problem.

The Lagrangian function is

$$\mathcal{L} = 2(x-2)^2 + \lambda\left(\frac{3}{2} - x\right).$$

The Kuhn–Tucker conditions are

$$\mathcal{L}_x = 4(x-2) - \lambda \geq 0, \quad x \geq 0, \quad x[4(x-2) - \lambda] = 0$$

$$\mathcal{L}_\lambda = \frac{3}{2} - x \leq 0, \qquad \lambda \geq 0, \quad \lambda\left(\frac{3}{2} - x\right) = 0.$$

Suppose that the constraint is binding, which implies that $\lambda > 0$ by complementary slackness. We obtain $x = 3/2$. Given that $x > 0$, we must have $\mathcal{L}_x = 0$. Substituting $x = 3/2$ into $\mathcal{L}_x = 0$ yields $\lambda = -2$. However, this value violates the non-negativity restriction $\lambda \geq 0$. Hence, it must be the case that $\lambda = 0$. Assuming $x > 0$, which implies $\mathcal{L}_x = 0$, we get $x = 2$. We can verify that the solution values $(x, \lambda) = (2, 0)$ satisfy the Kuhn–Tucker conditions. Thus, these values constitute the solution to the minimization problem.

(6.2) Consider a consumer who participates in two activities: fishing and diving. Her utility function is $U = 2F + D$, where F represents fishing and D represents diving. The consumer faces a time constraint given by $F+D \leq 8$ and a cash constraint of $F+2D \leq 10$. Use the Kuhn–Tucker conditions to find the solution to this problem.

Solution:

The consumer's problem is

$$\max_{F,D} U = 2F + D$$

$$\text{subject to } F + D \leq 8$$

$$F + 2D \leq 10$$

$$\text{and } F, D \geq 0.$$

The Lagrangian is

$$\mathcal{L} = 2F + D + \lambda_1(8 - F - D) + \lambda_2(10 - F - 2D).$$

The Kuhn–Tucker conditions are

$$\begin{aligned}
&\mathcal{L}_F = 2 - \lambda_1 - \lambda_2 \leq 0, && F \geq 0, && F(2 - \lambda_1 - \lambda_2) = 0\\
&\mathcal{L}_D = 1 - \lambda_1 - 2\lambda_2 \leq 0, && D \geq 0, && D(1 - \lambda_1 - 2\lambda_2) = 0\\
&\mathcal{L}_{\lambda_1} = 8 - F - D \geq 0, && \lambda_1 \geq 0, && \lambda_1(8 - F - D) = 0\\
&\mathcal{L}_{\lambda_2} = 10 - F - 2D \geq 0, && \lambda_2 \geq 0, && \lambda_2(10 - F - 2D) = 0.
\end{aligned}$$

We first assume that both constraints are binding, which implies that $\lambda_1 > 0$ and $\lambda_2 > 0$. Thus, we can write

$$\begin{aligned}
F + D &= 8,\\
F + 2D &= 10.
\end{aligned}$$

Solving this system of equations yields $F = 6$ and $D = 2$. Given that $F > 0$ and $D > 0$, we must have $\mathcal{L}_F = 0$ and $\mathcal{L}_D = 0$, leading to the equations

$$\begin{aligned}
\lambda_1 + \lambda_2 &= 2,\\
\lambda_1 + 2\lambda_2 &= 1.
\end{aligned}$$

These two equations yield the solution $\lambda_1 = 3$ and $\lambda_2 = -1$. However, this solution violates the non-negativity restriction $\lambda_2 \geq 0$. Hence, it must be that (i) either λ_1 or λ_2 is zero, and (ii) either F or D is zero.

Note that $\lambda_1 = \lambda_2 = 0$ does not have a meaningful interpretation, as the Lagrange multipliers represent the marginal utilities of relaxing the constraints. Similarly, having $F = D = 0$ would imply that $U = 0$, so this case can also be ruled out in our search for a solution. Accordingly, we have four possible cases: (a) $F > 0$, $D = 0$, $\lambda_1 > 0$ and $\lambda_2 = 0$; (b) $F > 0$, $D = 0$, $\lambda_1 = 0$ and $\lambda_2 > 0$;

(c) $F = 0$, $D > 0$, $\lambda_1 = 0$ and $\lambda_2 > 0$; and (d) $F = 0$, $D > 0$, $\lambda_1 > 0$ and $\lambda_2 = 0$.

Suppose that the first possibility is valid, namely $F > 0$, $D = 0$, $\lambda_1 > 0$ and $\lambda_2 = 0$. With $F > 0$ and $\lambda_1 > 0$, we can write

$$\lambda_1 + \lambda_2 = 2,$$
$$F + D = 8.$$

Given that $D = 0$ and $\lambda_2 = 0$, we get $\lambda_1 = 2$ and $F = 8$. Thus, we have the following set of trial solution values: $F = 8$, $D = 0$, $\lambda_1 = 2$ and $\lambda_2 = 0$. We can verify that these solution values satisfy the Kuhn–Tucker conditions. Further, this indicates that the trial solutions corresponding to the other three cases (b)–(d) will violate the Kuhn–Tucker conditions. For example, case (b) yields the solution $F = 10$, $D = 0$, $\lambda_1 = 0$ and $\lambda_2 = 2$, which, in turn, violates the condition $\mathcal{L}_{\lambda_1} = 8 - F - D \geq 0$. We conclude that the values $F = 8$, $D = 0$, $\lambda_1 = 2$ and $\lambda_2 = 0$ are the solution to this problem.

Further Reading

Arrow, K. J. & Enthoven, A. C. (1961). Quasi-Concave Programming. *Econometrica*, 29(4), 779–800.

Chiang, A. C. & Wainwright, K. (2005). *Fundamental Methods of Mathematical Economics*. Boston, McGraw-Hill.

Kuhn, H. W. & Tucker, A. W. (1951). Nonlinear programming, in J. Neyman (ed.), *Proceedings of the Second Berkeley Symposium on Mathematical Statistics and Probability*. University of California Press, Berkeley.

Luderer, B., Nollau, V., & Vetters, K. (2009). *Mathematical Formulas for Economists*. Berlin, Springer Science & Business Media.

Osborne, M. J. (2020, June 19). Mathematical Methods for Economic Theory. Retrieved from https://mjo.osborne.economics.utoronto.ca/index.php/tutorial/index/1/int/i.

Silberberg, E. & Suen, W. (2000). *The Structure of Economics: A Mathematical Analysis*. Boston, McGraw-Hill.

Simon, C. P. & Blume, L. (1994). *Mathematics for Economists*. New York, Norton.

Varian, H. R. (1992). *Microeconomics Analysis* (third edition). New York, Norton.

CHAPTER 7

INTEGRAL CALCULUS

Learning Objectives

After completing this chapter, students will be able to:

- Apply rules of integration to find specific integrals.
- Recognize the circumstances under which the basic rules of integration cannot be applied, and where the substitution rule or integration by parts may be more suitable.
- Understand the concept of a definite integral and its properties.
- Evaluate improper integrals, including those with infinite limits of integration and those with infinite integrands.

In the static models of Chapters 5 and 6, our goal was to maximize or minimize an objective function subject to one or more constraints. The first-order conditions characterized the optimal solution and served as equilibrium conditions. In this chapter, we will develop additional tools of economic analysis before shifting our focus to solving various differential equations. In dynamic analysis, we will study the time paths of variables and determine whether, given sufficient time, they converge to particular values.[1]

Starting with a pattern of change and tracing a time path essentially requires uncovering the primitive function from a derived function. In simple cases, this can be accomplished using integral calculus, which is, generally speaking, the reverse process of differentiation studied in Chapter 2. Just as there are rules for differentiation, there are also rules for integration that we will study in this chapter.

7.1 The Concept of Integration

To fix ideas, we start our discussion of integrals and the process of integration with an example. Consider a herd of horses that changes over time at the rate of

$$\frac{dH}{dt} = \frac{1}{2}t^{\frac{1}{4}}.$$

Given this instantaneous rate of change, our objective is to find the function $H = H(t)$. $H(t)$ is called the *primitive* function and, in simple cases like the one considered here, can be found using integration. In other words, starting from a *derived* function, $(1/2)t^{1/4}$, we seek to find the primitive function. In this respect, integration is the reverse process of differentiation.

More generally, let $f(x)$ be the primitive function and $f'(x)$ be the derived function. The underlying idea is simple: if differentiating

[1] See, however, the discussion in Arrow and Hahn (1971, p. 245) on why the conventional distinction between *statics* and *dynamics* may be misleading. Arrow and Hahn suggest that in economies with futures markets, it is challenging to categorize situations strictly as static or dynamic. On the one hand, contracts in futures markets are created at a specific moment, which is consistent with static analysis. On the other hand, the quantities of goods produced and stored can change over time as conditions evolve, which is consistent with dynamic analysis.

the primitive function yields the derived function, then integrating the derived function allows us to obtain the primitive function. Specifically,

$$\frac{d}{dx}f(x) = f'(x).$$

Integrating the function $f'(x)$ yields the primitive function $f(x)$ as follows:

$$\int f'(x)dx = f(x) + c.$$

The elongated S symbol denotes the integral; $f'(x)$ is the function to be integrated, known as the *integrand*; and c is an arbitrary constant of integration. Given that c is arbitrary, we require additional information to determine its value. Such information typically comes in the form of an initial condition.

In our example, the rate of change of the herd of horses over time is

$$\frac{dH}{dt} = \frac{1}{2}t^{\frac{1}{4}}.$$

Notice that if we differentiate the function $H(t) = (2/5)t^{5/4}$, we obtain the derivative $(1/2)t^{1/4}$. However, there are many other functions, such as $H(t) = (2/5)t^{5/4} + 10$, with the same derivative or, more generally, $H(t) = (2/5)t^{5/4} + c$. Hence, we need to identify the arbitrary constant c. Consider the initial condition $H(0) = 20$. This provides the value of H at time $t = 0$, leading to the equation

$$H(0) = \frac{2}{5}t^{\frac{5}{4}} + c = 20.$$

Solving for c yields $c = 20$. Thus, $H(t) = (2/5)t^{5/4} + 20$, given the initial condition $H(0) = 20$.

To summarize, we have established that integration is the reverse process of differentiation. When we differentiate a function $f(x)$ with respect to x, we obtain the function $f'(x)$. Then, integrating $f'(x)$ with respect to x allows us to recover the primitive function $f(x)$. Since there is no definite numerical value for the integral $\int f'(x)dx$ (even if the value of c can be specified), it is referred to as an *indefinite integral.* The reason we cannot find an exact value is that the expression $f(x) + c$ varies with the value of x. In other words, the integral has no upper or lower bounds. Later in this chapter, we will discuss the case of a *definite integral,* where the integral does indeed have bounds. Just as there are rules for differentiation, there are also rules that can simplify the process of integration, which we consider in the following section.

7.2 Basic Rules of Integration

7.2.1 *Rule I: The power rule*

The power rule of integration is the reverse of the power rule of differentiation. This means that if the integration process is performed correctly, differentiating the primitive function will yield the integrand x^n. The power rule can thus be stated as follows:

$$\int x^n dx = \frac{x^{n+1}}{n+1} + c, \quad n \neq -1.$$

Example: Find $\int x^5 dx$.

Given that $n = 5$, applying the power rule yields

$$\int x^5 dx = \frac{x^6}{6} + c,$$

where c is an arbitrary constant.

Example: Find $\int 1dx$.

Here, $n = 0$ because $x^0 = 1$. Thus, we have

$$\int 1dx = x + c.$$

Note that $\int 1dx$ can also be expressed as $\int dx$.

7.2.2 *Rule II: The logarithmic rule*

$$\int \frac{1}{x}dx = \ln x + c, \quad x > 0.$$

Notice that this rule is not applicable for all values of x. The restriction is that x must always be positive because logarithms are undefined for non-positive values. Therefore, we can also write the aforementioned equation as

$$\int \frac{1}{x}dx = \ln|x| + c, \quad x \neq 0.$$

Note that

$$\frac{d}{dx}\ln|x| = \frac{1}{x}.$$

More generally, the logarithmic rule can be stated in terms of a function $a(x)$ as

$$\int \frac{a'(x)}{a(x)}dx = \ln a(x) + c, \quad a(x) > 0.$$

This suggests that the integral of the derivative of a function divided by the function itself yields the logarithm of the function plus an arbitrary constant. To account for possible negative values of $a(x)$, we can write

$$\int \frac{a'(x)}{a(x)}dx = \ln|a(x)| + c, \quad a(x) \neq 0.$$

7.2.3 *Rule III: The exponential rule*

$$\int e^x dx = e^x + c.$$

Moreover, we have

$$\int a'(x)e^{a(x)} dx = e^{a(x)} + c.$$

It is straightforward to verify that the derivative of the primitive function is equal to the integrand.

7.2.4 *Rule IV: The sum-difference rule*

The integral of the sum (or difference) of a given number of functions is equal to sum (or difference) of the integrals of the respective functions. That is

$$\int [a(x) \pm b(x)]dx = \int a(x)dx \pm \int b(x)dx.$$

This rule is useful because it allows us to handle more complicated integrals than those encountered so far, as the following example illustrates.

Example: Find $\int (4e^{4x} + \frac{6x}{3x^2+5})dx$.

We know from the sum-difference rule that the integral of the sum is the sum of the integrals. Thus, we have

$$\int \left(4e^{4x} + \frac{6x}{3x^2+5}\right) dx = \int 4e^{4x} dx + \int \frac{6x}{3x^2+5} dx.$$

Using the exponential rule to calculate the first integral and the logarithmic rule to calculate the second, we obtain

$$e^{4x} + c_1 + \ln(3x^2+5) + c_2 = e^{4x} + \ln(3x^2+5) + c.$$

In the final answer, the two constants have been combined into a single constant c.

7.2.5 *Rule V: The multiplication by a constant rule*

$$\int ka(x)dx = k\int a(x)dx.$$

This rule states that the constant k can be factored out of the integral. This is because k does not depend on the variable of integration x, so that the integral of k times the integrand $a(x)$ is k times the integral of $a(x)$.

Example: Find $\int 2x^3dx$.

Here, $k = 2$ and this can be factored out of the integral as follows:

$$\int 2x^3dx = 2\int x^3dx.$$

Applying the power rule, we obtain

$$2\int x^3dx = 2\frac{x^4}{4} + c = \frac{1}{2}x^4 + c.$$

The correctness of the answer can again be verified by differentiation.

7.3 Rules Involving Substitution

We consider two additional rules that may help simplify the integration process through the substitution of the original variable of integration with a new variable. These rules may be applicable whenever the rules studied so far do not provide an answer to the integral we wish to calculate.

7.3.1 *Rule VI: The substitution rule*

The essence of the substitution rule is to rewrite a function of a variable x in terms of a new variable u. Let $g(u)$ be the primitive function where $u = u(x)$. The substitution rule can be stated as

$$\int f(x)dx = \int g'(u)du = g(u) + c,$$

where the integrand $f(x)$ is equal to $g'(u)(\frac{du}{dx})$.

A proof of this result is fairly straightforward. It starts by recognizing that the substitution rule is the reverse application of the chain rule of differentiation, which tells us how to find the derivative of a composite function; $g(u(x))$ is such a composite function. For simplicity, let $P(x) = g(u(x))$. From the chain rule, we have

$$P'(x) = g'(u(x))u'(x),$$

Integrating both sides of this equation yields

$$P(x) = \int g'(u(x))\frac{du}{dx}dx,$$

which simplifies to

$$\int g'(u)du = g(u) + c.$$

Thus, the proof is complete.

Example: Find $\int 3\sqrt{x}dx$.

Letting $u = \sqrt{x}$, we can find du as follows:

$$du = \frac{1}{2\sqrt{x}}dx.$$

Solving for dx gives $dx = 2\sqrt{x}du$. Given that $u = \sqrt{x}$, we can express dx in terms of u, $dx = 2udu$. Substituting $u = \sqrt{x}$ and $dx = 2udu$ into the integral, we have

$$\int 3\sqrt{x}dx = \int 3u2udu = 6\int u^2du = 2u^3 + c.$$

Substituting $\sqrt{x}$ back into u gives us

$$\int 3\sqrt{x}dx = 2x^{\frac{3}{2}} + c.$$

7.3.2 *Rule VII: Integration by parts*

This rule states that the integral of v with respect to u is equal to the product of u and v minus the integral of u with respect to v

$$\int g(x)f'(x)dx = f(x)g(x) - \int f(x)g'(x)dx$$

or

$$\int vdu = uv - \int udv,$$

where $u = f(x)$ and $v = g(x)$. The main idea of this rule is to replace the operation $\int du$ with $\int dv$. To better understand integration by parts, we note that the product rule of differentials indicates

$$d(uv) = vdu + udv.$$

Integrating both sides yields

$$\int d(uv) = \int vdu + \int udv.$$

This leads to

$$uv = \int vdu + \int udv.$$

Rearranging the terms produces the desired result.

Example: Find $\int x\sqrt{x+2}dx$.

Let $v = x$ and $du = \sqrt{x+2}dx$; then $dv = dx$. Before applying integration by parts, we need to find u, which is the primitive function of du

$$u = \frac{2}{3}(x+2)^{\frac{3}{2}}.$$

Thus, we have

$$\int x\sqrt{x+2}\,dx = \int v\,du = uv - \int u\,dv.$$

Substituting u, v, and dv into the equation gives us

$$\frac{2}{3}(x+2)^{\frac{3}{2}}x - \int \frac{2}{3}(x+2)^{\frac{3}{2}}dx.$$

Calculating the integral leads to

$$\frac{2}{3}x(x+2)^{\frac{3}{2}} - \frac{4}{15}(x+2)^{\frac{5}{2}} + c.$$

Thus, we can write

$$\int x\sqrt{x+2}\,dx = \frac{2}{3}x(x+2)^{\frac{3}{2}} - \frac{4}{15}(x+2)^{\frac{5}{2}} + c.$$

Example: Find $\int \ln(x^2)dx$.

Let $v = \ln(x^2)$ and $du = dx$; then $dv = (2/x)dx$ and $u = x$. Substituting into the integration by parts formula, we obtain

$$\int \ln(x^2)dx = x\ln(x^2) - \int x\frac{2}{x}dx = x\ln(x^2) - 2x + c.$$

The correctness of the answer can be verified by differentiation.

Example: Find $\int 3x^2(x^3+5)dx$.

Let $v = 3x^2$ and $du = (x^3+5)dx$; then $dv = 6xdx$ and $u = x^4/4 + 5x$. It follows that

$$\int 3x^2(x^3+5)dx = \left(\frac{x^4}{4} + 5x\right)3x^2 - \int \left(\frac{x^4}{4} + 5x\right)6xdx.$$

This simplifies to

$$\frac{3x^6}{4} + 15x^3 - \frac{x^6}{4} - 10x^3 + c = \frac{1}{2}x^6 + 5x^3 + c.$$

7.4 Definite Integrals: The Area under a Curve

So far, our focus has been on indefinite integrals, which do not have a specific numerical value as they represent functions of a variable. In contrast, the definite integral of a function has a specific value and can be defined as follows:

$$\int_{\alpha}^{\beta} a(x)dx = A(x)|_{\alpha}^{\beta} = A(\beta) - A(\alpha),$$

where α is the *lower limit of integration* and β is the *upper limit of intcgration.*

Example: Evaluate $\int_1^4 xdx$.

First, we find the corresponding indefinite integral

$$\int xdx = \frac{1}{2}x^2 + c.$$

Evaluating the indefinite integral at the given limits of integration gives us

$$\int_1^4 xdx = \left.\frac{1}{2}x^2\right]_1^4 = \frac{1}{2}(16 - 1) = 7.5.$$

Example: Evaluate $\int_0^1 (2x + \frac{16x}{8x^2+5})dx$.

The indefinite integral is given by $x^2 + \ln(8x^2 + 5) + c$. Therefore, we can write the definite integral as

$$\int_0^1 \left(2x + \frac{16x}{8x^2 + 5}\right) dx = [x^2 + \ln(8x^2 + 5)]_0^1.$$

Evaluating at $x = 1$

$$1 + \ln(8 + 5).$$

Evaluating at $x = 0$

$$0 + \ln(0 + 5).$$

Combining these results gives us

$$\left[x^2 + \ln\left(8x^2 + 5\right)\right]_0^1 = 1 + \ln 13 - \ln 5.$$

Thus, we obtain the result

$$\int_0^1 \left(2x + \frac{16x}{8x^2 + 5}\right) dx = 1 + \ln 13 - \ln 5.$$

To illustrate the concept of the definite integral, we use a diagram. Graphically, the definite integral represents the area under a given curve. Consider the continuous function $y = f(x)$ displayed in Figure 7.1. Suppose we want to measure the shaded area

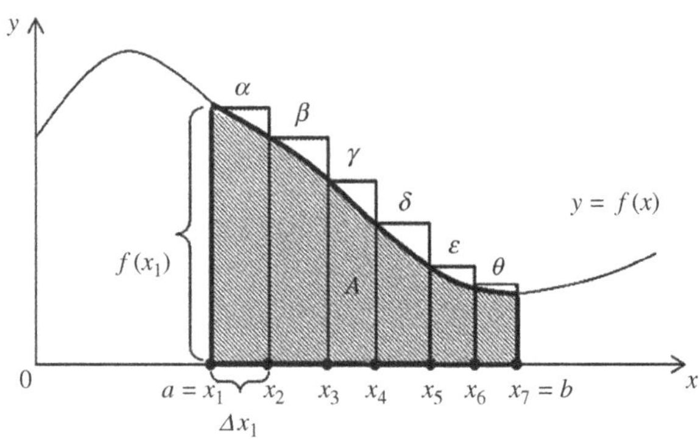

Figure 7.1

A, which lies under the function $f(x)$ and above the horizontal axis x. One way to measure this area is by dividing it into rectangular blocks, such as those shown in the figure: α, β, and so on, up to θ. Summing the areas of these rectangular blocks provides an approximation of the shaded area A. To be more precise, we divide the interval $[a, b]$ into $n = 6$ subintervals (not necessarily of equal length) along the x-axis: $[x_1, x_2], [x_2, x_3], \ldots, [x_6, x_7]$. On each subinterval, we consider a rectangular block. Since each subinterval reflects a change in x, we denote it as Δx_i. Thus, we obtain an approximation of the shaded area A as $A^* = \sum_{i=1}^{n=6} f(x_i)\Delta x_i$.

It should be noted that using A^* will overestimate A because the unshaded areas in the rectangles above the curve are also included when measuring A^*. To address this overestimation, we apply finer and finer segmentation of the area A, making the unshaded areas smaller and smaller, thus bringing A^* closer to the actual area it is intended to approximate. This implies that, in the limit as $n \to \infty$, A^* will converge to A. Accordingly, we can write

$$\lim_{n\to\infty} \sum_{i=1}^{n} f(x_i)\Delta x_i = \lim_{n\to\infty} A^* = \text{area } A.$$

Noting that $\int_a^b$ is the continuous counterpart of the discrete sum $\sum_{i=1}^{n}$, we can express the area A as

$$\text{area } A = \int_a^b f(x)dx = F(b) - F(a),$$

where $F(x)$ is the primitive function of $f(x)$. Taken together, these equations suggest that a definite integral can be defined as the area under a given curve.

7.5 Properties of Definite Integrals

We now state some properties of definite integrals.

7.5.1 *Property I: Interchanging the limits of integration*

By multiplying the integral by a minus sign, the upper (lower) limit becomes the lower (upper) limit and vice versa. In other words, the two limits of integration are interchanged. That is

$$\int_a^b a(x)dx = -\int_b^a a(x)dx.$$

A proof of this result is as follows. We have

$$\int_a^b a(x)dx = A(b) - A(a).$$

This equation can be rewritten as

$$-[A(a) - A(b)] = -\int_b^a a(x)dx.$$

7.5.2 *Property II: Identical limits of integration*

If the upper and lower limits of integration are identical, the value of the definite integral is zero

$$\int_a^a a(x)dx = 0.$$

To see this, note that

$$\int_a^a a(x)dx = A(a) - A(a) = 0.$$

7.5.3 *Property III: Sum of definite integrals*

The integral over an interval can be expressed as the sum of integrals over subintervals

$$\int_{\alpha}^{\varepsilon} a(x)dx = \int_{\alpha}^{\beta} a(x)dx + \int_{\beta}^{\gamma} a(x)dx + \int_{\gamma}^{\delta} a(x)dx + \int_{\delta}^{\varepsilon} a(x)dx.$$

where $\alpha < \beta < \gamma < \delta < \varepsilon$. This property, known as the additivity property, extends to a finite number of subintervals, not just the four mentioned. Specifically, it applies to intervals $(\alpha, \beta)(\beta, \gamma), \ldots,$ $(n-1, n)$. Moreover, it is important to note that both continuous and discontinuous functions can be integrated. For example, consider the step function displayed in Figure 7.2(a). This function exhibits discontinuities at points β and γ. Despite this, we can find the shaded area under the function as

$$\int_{\alpha}^{\beta} a(x)dx + \int_{\beta}^{\gamma} a(x)dx + \int_{\gamma}^{\delta} a(x)dx.$$

Additionally, we can state that

$$\int_{\alpha}^{\beta} [a(x) + b(x)]dx = \int_{\alpha}^{\beta} a(x)dx + \int_{\alpha}^{\beta} b(x)dx.$$

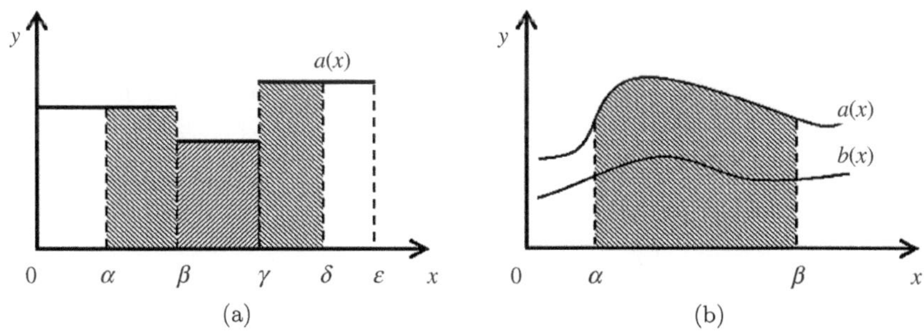

Figure 7.2

This property is similar to the summation rule of indefinite integrals that we studied earlier. It suggests that the definite integral of a sum of two (or more) functions is the sum of the definite integrals of the respective functions (see Figure 7.2(b)).

Finally, the multiplication by a constant rule as well as integration by parts can be extended to the case of definite integrals as follows:

$$\int_{\alpha}^{\beta} ka(x)dx = k\int_{\alpha}^{\beta} a(x)dx,$$

$$\int_{\alpha}^{\beta} vdu = uv|_{\alpha}^{\beta} - \int_{\alpha}^{\beta} udv.$$

7.6 Improper Integrals

A definite integral is said to be *improper* if either the upper or lower limit of integration is infinite. It can also be considered as improper if the integrand is found to be infinite, even if the limits of integration are finite. In this section, we examine two cases of improper integrals: (i) integrals where one of the limits of integration is infinite; and (ii) integrals where the integrand becomes infinite within the integration interval.

7.6.1 *Infinite limit of integration*

Suppose that the upper (or lower) limit of integration is infinite, that is

$$\int_{\alpha}^{\infty} a(x)dx \quad \text{and} \quad \int_{-\infty}^{\beta} a(x)dx.$$

In these two cases, we cannot directly evaluate the integrals, as this would require calculating $A(\infty)-A(\alpha)$ and $A(\beta)-A(-\infty)$, respectively. This issue arises because ∞ is not a number and cannot be substituted into the function $A(x)$. Therefore, we apply the concept of the limit as follows:

$$\int_{\alpha}^{\infty} a(x)dx = \lim_{\beta\to\infty} \int_{\alpha}^{\beta} a(x)dx.$$

Similarly, if the lower limit of integration is infinite, we can write

$$\int_{-\infty}^{\beta} a(x)dx = \lim_{\alpha\to-\infty} \int_{\alpha}^{\beta} a(x)dx.$$

Evaluating the limit, two types of outcomes can arise. An improper integral is said to be *convergent* if the limit exists (i.e., it is finite). Conversely, if the limit does not exist, the improper integral is said to be *divergent*, and it does not have a meaningful interpretation.

Example: Evaluate $\int_2^\infty \frac{dx}{x^3}$.

We begin by noting that

$$\int_2^\infty \frac{dx}{x^3} = \lim_{\beta\to\infty} \int_2^\beta \frac{dx}{x^3}.$$

Next, we calculate the definite integral

$$\int_2^\beta \frac{dx}{x^3} = -\frac{1}{2x^2}\bigg|_2^\beta = -\frac{1}{2}\left(\frac{1}{\beta^2} - \frac{1}{4}\right).$$

Taking the limit as $\beta \to \infty$, we obtain

$$\lim_{\beta\to\infty} \int_2^\beta \frac{dx}{x^3} = \lim_{\beta\to\infty} -\frac{1}{2}\left(\frac{1}{\beta^2} - \frac{1}{4}\right) = \frac{1}{8}.$$

The integral has the value of $1/8$ and therefore it converges.

7.6.2 *Infinite integrand*

Even if the limits of integration are finite, an integral can still be improper if the integrand becomes infinite at some point within the interval of integration $[\alpha, \beta]$. To illustrate, consider the following example.

Example: Evaluate $\int_0^5 \frac{dx}{x}$.

The function $\frac{1}{x}$ approaches ∞ as $x \to 0^+$, so we define the integral using a limit

$$\int_0^5 \frac{dx}{x} = \lim_{\alpha \to 0^+} \int_\alpha^5 \frac{dx}{x}.$$

Evaluating the integral

$$\int_\alpha^5 \frac{dx}{x} = \ln x|_\alpha^5 = \ln 5 - \ln \alpha.$$

where $\alpha > 0$. Then, we evaluate the limit as $\alpha \to 0^+$

$$\lim_{\alpha \to 0^+} (\ln 5 - \ln \alpha).$$

Note that $\ln \alpha \to -\infty$ as $\alpha \to 0^+$. Given that the limit is infinite, the improper integral is divergent.

7.7 Further Exercises and Applications

(7.1) Find $\int \sqrt{x^2} dx$.

Solution:

Because the square root function satisfies $\sqrt{x^2} = |x|$, it is necessary to consider the cases $x \geq 0$ and $x < 0$ separately.

Case 1: $x \geq 0$

$$\int x\, dx = \frac{x^2}{2} + c.$$

Case 2: $x < 0$

$$\int -x\, dx = -\frac{x^2}{2} + c.$$

Thus, applying the power rule yields

$$\int \sqrt{x^2}dx = \begin{cases} -\frac{x^2}{2} + c, & x < 0 \\ \frac{x^2}{2} + c, & x \geq 0 \end{cases}.$$

(7.2) Provide a proof of the multiplication rule of integration

$$\int ka(x)dx = k\int a(x)dx,$$

where k is a constant.

Solution:

To show this result, we begin from the left-hand side of the equation and demonstrate that it is equal to the right-hand side. We can rewrite the left-hand side as

$$\int \left[\underbrace{a(x) + \cdots + a(x)}_{k \text{ terms}}\right] dx.$$

Using summation notation

$$\int \sum_{i=1}^{k} a(x)dx.$$

By the linearity of integration, we can write the summation outside the integral

$$\sum_{i=1}^{k} \int a(x)dx.$$

Since the integral of $a(x)$ appears k times, this simplifies to

$$k\int a(x)dx.$$

Thus, we have shown that

$$\int ka(x)dx = \sum_{i=1}^{k} \int a(x)dx = k \int a(x)dx.$$

This completes the proof of the multiplication by a constant rule of integration.

(7.3) Find $\int 3x^2(x^3 + 5)dx$.

Solution:

Using the substitution rule, let $u = x^3 + 5$; then $du = 3x^2 dx$. Solving for dx yields

$$dx = \frac{du}{3x^2}.$$

Substitution of u for $x^3 + 5$ and dx for $du/3x^2$ gives

$$\int 3x^2(x^3 + 5)dx = \int 3x^2 u \frac{du}{3x^2} = \int u\, du.$$

Then, applying the power rule

$$\int u\, du = \frac{u^2}{2} + c_1.$$

Substituting back for u, we have

$$\frac{1}{2}\left(x^3 + 5\right)^2 + c_1.$$

Since c_1 is an arbitrary constant of integration, it can be rewritten as a general constant c by absorbing any numerical terms that appear due to expansion. Thus, we redefine

$$c = c_1 + 12.5.$$

The result can be written as

$$\frac{1}{2}(x^3+5)^2+c_1=\frac{1}{2}x^6+5x^3+c.$$

Notice that the same answer can also be reached by first multiplying out the integrand and then applying the sum rule of integration

$$\int 3x^2(x^3+5)dx=\int (3x^5+15x^2)dx=\int 3x^5dx+\int 15x^2dx$$
$$=\frac{1}{2}x^6+5x^3+c.$$

(7.4) Find $\int \frac{(\ln x)^2}{x}dx$.

Solution:

Using the substitution rule, let $u=\ln x$. We have $du=\frac{1}{x}dx$, which implies that $dx=xdu$. Thus, we can express the integral as follows:

$$\int \frac{(\ln x)^2}{x}dx=\int \frac{u^2}{x}xdu=\int u^2du.$$

Calculating the integral, we obtain

$$\int u^2du=\frac{u^3}{3}+c.$$

Substituting back $u=\ln x$, we arrive at the final result

$$\int \frac{(\ln x)^2}{x}dx=\frac{(\ln x)^3}{3}+c.$$

(7.5) Find $\int (\ln x)^2dx$.

Solution:

To find this integral, we apply integration by parts. Let

$$v=(\ln x)^2 \quad \text{and} \quad du=dx.$$

Differentiating v and integrating du yields

$$dv = \left(\frac{2}{x}\right) \ln x dx \quad \text{and} \quad u = x.$$

Using integration by parts

$$\int (\ln x)^2 dx = x(\ln x)^2 - \int x \frac{2}{x} \ln x dx.$$

Simplifying

$$\int (\ln x)^2 dx = x(\ln x)^2 - 2 \int \ln x dx.$$

Next, we apply integration by parts again to evaluate $\int \ln x dx$. Let

$$v = \ln x \quad \text{and} \quad du = dx.$$

Then

$$dv = \left(\frac{1}{x}\right) dx \quad \text{and} \quad u = x.$$

Applying integration by parts

$$\int \ln x dx = x \ln x - x + c_1.$$

Using this result, we obtain

$$\int (\ln x)^2 dx = x(\ln x)^2 - 2(x \ln x - x + c_1).$$

Expanding leads to

$$x(\ln x)^2 - 2x \ln x + 2x - 2c_1.$$

Thus, we can write

$$\int (\ln x)^2 dx = x(\ln x)^2 - 2x(\ln x - 1) + c,$$

where we have substituted the arbitrary constant $-2c_1$ for the general constant c.

(7.6) Evaluate $\int_0^\infty \frac{5}{(x+1)^{3/2}}dx$.

Solution:

Using the substitution method, let $u = x + 1$; then, $du = dx$. Rewriting the integral in terms of u, we have (omitting the concept of the limit)

$$\int_0^\infty \frac{5}{(x+1)^{3/2}}dx = \int_1^\infty \frac{5}{u^{3/2}}du.$$

We first evaluate

$$\int \frac{5}{u^{3/2}}du.$$

Rewriting the exponent

$$\int 5u^{-3/2}du.$$

Applying the power rule

$$\frac{5}{-1/2}u^{-1/2} = -10u^{-1/2}.$$

Rewriting

$$-10\frac{1}{\sqrt{u}}.$$

Evaluating from $u = 1$ to $u = \infty$

$$\left.\frac{-10}{\sqrt{u}}\right]_1^\infty.$$

It follows that

$$\left.\frac{-10}{\sqrt{u}}\right]_1^\infty = \lim_{\beta\to\infty}\left(\frac{-10}{\sqrt{\beta}}\right) - \left(\frac{-10}{\sqrt{1}}\right),$$

where $\lim_{\beta\to\infty}(\frac{-10}{\sqrt{\beta}}) = 0$. Finally, we get

$$\lim_{\beta\to\infty}\left(\frac{-10}{\sqrt{\beta}}\right) - \left(\frac{-10}{\sqrt{1}}\right) = 0 + 10 = 10.$$

The integral converges and has the specific numerical value of 10.

(7.7) Evaluate $\int_1^\infty \frac{\ln x}{2x^2}dx$.

Solution:

Factoring out the 1/2, we rewrite the integral as

$$\frac{1}{2}\int_1^\infty \frac{\ln x}{x^2}dx.$$

We use integration by parts

$$v = \ln x \Rightarrow dv = \left(\frac{1}{x}\right)dx,$$

$$du = \left(\frac{1}{x^2}\right)dx \Rightarrow u = -\frac{1}{x}.$$

Applying integration by parts leads to

$$\int \frac{\ln x}{x^2}dx = -\frac{\ln x}{x} + \int \frac{1}{x^2}dx = -\frac{\ln x}{x} - \frac{1}{x}.$$

Applying limits from $x = 1$ to $x = \infty$

$$\frac{1}{2}\left(-\frac{\ln x}{x} - \frac{1}{x}\right)\Big]_1^\infty.$$

Substituting $x = \infty$

$$\lim_{\beta\to\infty}\frac{1}{2}\left(-\frac{\ln\beta}{\beta} - \frac{1}{\beta}\right).$$

Substituting $x = 1$

$$\frac{1}{2}\left(\frac{-\ln 1}{1} - \frac{1}{1}\right) = \frac{1}{2}(0 - 1) = -\frac{1}{2}.$$

To evaluate $\lim_{\beta\to\infty} \frac{\ln\beta}{\beta}$, we note this limit approaches the indeterminate form $\frac{\infty}{\infty}$, so we apply L'Hospital's rule

$$\lim_{\beta\to\infty} \frac{\ln\beta}{\beta} = \lim_{\beta\to\infty} \frac{1/\beta}{1}.$$

Given that

$$\lim_{\beta\to\infty} \frac{1}{\beta} = 0,$$

we obtain

$$\lim_{\beta\to\infty} \frac{1}{2}\left(-\frac{\ln\beta}{\beta} - \frac{1}{\beta}\right) = \frac{1}{2}(0-0) = 0.$$

Combining the results, we compute the final value of the integral

$$\begin{aligned}\int_1^{\infty} \frac{\ln x}{2x^2} dx &= \lim_{\beta\to\infty} \frac{1}{2}\left(-\frac{\ln\beta}{\beta} - \frac{1}{\beta}\right) - \frac{1}{2}(-\ln 1 - 1) \\ &= \frac{1}{2}(0-0) + \frac{1}{2}(1) = \frac{1}{2}.\end{aligned}$$

The improper integral has the value of $1/2$ and hence it converges.

Further Reading

Arrow, K. J. & Hahn, F. H. (1971). *General Competitive Analysis.* San Francisco, Holden-Day.

Chiang, A. C. & Wainwright, K. (2005). *Fundamental Methods of Mathematical Economics.* Boston, McGraw-Hill.

Luderer, B., Nollau, V., & Vetters, K. (2009). *Mathematical Formulas for Economists.* Berlin, Springer Science & Business Media.

Silberberg, E. & Suen, W. (2000). *The Structure of Economics: A Mathematical Analysis.* Boston, McGraw-Hill.

Simon, C. P. & Blume, L. (1994). *Mathematics for Economists.* New York, Norton.

Sydsaeter, K., Hammond, P., Seierstad, A. & Strom, A. (2008). *Further Mathematics for Economic Analysis* (second edition). Harlow, Pearson.

CHAPTER 8

ECONOMIC DYNAMICS AND FIRST-ORDER LINEAR DIFFERENTIAL EQUATIONS

Learning Objectives

After completing this chapter, students will be able to:

- Understand the concept of a first-order linear differential equation.
- Solve differential equations with a constant coefficient and a constant term.
- Solve differential equations with a variable coefficient and a variable term.
- Verify the solutions of different types of differential equations.
- Appreciate how differential equations can be useful in understanding the dynamics of certain economic variables, including market prices.

In Chapter 7, we developed tools for economic analysis related to integral calculus. We are now ready to tackle problems involving differential equations. In this chapter, we will study the time path of a variable to determine whether, given sufficient time, it converges to a specific equilibrium value. Unlike Chapters 5 and 6, where we focused on static optimization problems, we will not assume that an equilibrium exists *a priori*. Instead, we will begin by considering a pattern of change that describes the behavior of a variable over time. We will then examine the adjustment process toward a specific value and determine whether an equilibrium exists.

8.1 The Concept of First-Order Linear Differential Equations

Consider a function of a dependent variable y that varies with respect to an independent variable t. Further, consider a differential equation consisting of three terms: the derivative of y with respect to t, the product of y and a coefficient a, and an additional term b. An equation of this form is referred to as a differential equation. The *degree* of the differential equation is the highest power of the derivative dy/dt. If both y and its derivative dy/dt are of the first degree, and there is no product of the form $y(dy/dt)$, the equation is said to be a *first-order linear differential equation*, represented as

$$\frac{dy}{dt} + ay = b. \tag{8.1}$$

The constants a and b can also be continuous functions of t

$$\frac{dy}{dt} + a(t)y = b(t). \tag{8.2}$$

Equation (8.1) is a first-order linear differential equation with a constant coefficient and a constant term, whereas (8.2) is a differential equation of the same type but with a variable coefficient $a(t)$ and a variable term $b(t)$.

8.2 Constant Coefficient and Constant Term

8.2.1 *The homogeneous case*

A first-order linear differential equation with a constant coefficient and a constant term takes the form of (8.1). In the special case where $b = 0$, the equation becomes

$$\frac{dy}{dt} + ay = 0, \tag{8.3}$$

which is referred to as the *homogeneous* case. In general, the solution to this equation is given by

$$y(t) = Ae^{-at}. \tag{8.4}$$

We now derive this solution. Equation (8.3) can be rewritten as

$$\frac{dy}{dt} = -ay,$$

or, equivalently,

$$\frac{1}{y}\frac{dy}{dt} = -a.$$

Integrating both sides

$$\int \frac{1}{y}\frac{dy}{dt}dt = -\int adt.$$

Calculating the integrals, we obtain

$$\ln y + c_1 = -at + c_2,$$

with $y > 0$. Letting $c_2 - c_1 \equiv c$, the equation simplifies to

$$\ln y = -at + c.$$

Given that $e^{\ln y} = y$, we take the antilog of $\ln y$

$$e^{\ln y} = e^{-at+c}.$$

This gives us the general solution

$$y(t) = Ae^{-at},$$

where $A \equiv e^c$. The following theorem summarizes this result.

Theorem 1: The general solution to the homogeneous first-order linear differential equation $\frac{dy}{dt} + ay = 0$ is $y(t) = Ae^{-at}$, where A is an arbitrary constant and a is a constant coefficient with $a \neq 0$.

We proceed to definitize the arbitrary constant A. Consider the initial condition at the beginning of the time path of y (when $t = 0$) and substitute it into the general solution

$$y(0) = Ae^0.$$

Given that $e^0 = 1$, we have

$$y(0) = A.$$

Substituting $y(0)$ for A into the solution yields

$$y(t) = y(0)e^{-at}.$$

The following theorem summarizes this result.

Theorem 2: The definite solution to the homogeneous first-order linear differential equation $\frac{dy}{dt} + ay = 0$ is $y(t) = y(0)e^{-at}$, where a is a constant coefficient with $a \neq 0$.

Example: Solve the equation $\frac{dy}{dt} + 8y = 0$ with the initial condition $y(0) = 100$.

From Theorem 2, we know that the definite solution is

$$y(t) = y(0)e^{-at}.$$

In our case, $a = 8$ and $y(0) = 100$. Substituting these values gives us

$$y(t) = 100e^{-8t}.$$

8.2.2 *The non-homogeneous case*

When the coefficient a and the term b are both non-zero arbitrary constants, a first-order linear differential equation is said to be *non-homogeneous* and is written as

$$\frac{dy}{dt} + ay = b. \tag{8.5}$$

Equation (8.3) is known as the *reduced equation*, whereas (8.5) is referred to as the *complete equation*. We can find the solution to the non-homogeneous equation by considering additional steps in the solution process used for the homogeneous case. The solution consists of two parts: the complementary function (denoted by y_c) and the particular integral (denoted by y_p). Thus, the solution to the complete equation is given by

$$y(t) = y_c + y_p. \tag{8.6}$$

The complementary function y_c is the general solution to the reduced (or homogeneous) equation and takes the form Ae^{-at}. The particular integral y_p is any specific solution to the complete Equation (8.5). Substituting (8.6) into (8.5) gives

$$\frac{d(y_c + y_p)}{dt} + a(y_c + y_p) = b.$$

Using the complementary function $y_c = Ae^{-at}$

$$\frac{d(Ae^{-at} + y_p)}{dt} + a(Ae^{-at} + y_p) = b.$$

Simplifying the equation

$$-aAe^{-at} + \frac{dy_p}{dt} + aAe^{-at} + ay_p = b.$$

Next, consider the simplest possible solution for y_p, which is a constant ($y_p = k$). This implies that

$$\frac{dy_p}{dt} = 0.$$

Thus, we find

$$y_p = \frac{b}{a}.$$

Theorem 3: The general solution to the non-homogeneous first-order linear differential equation $\frac{dy}{dt} + ay = b$ is $y(t) = Ae^{-at} + \frac{b}{a}$, where A is an arbitrary constant, a is a constant coefficient with $a \neq 0$, and b is a constant term.

The next step is to definitize A. By letting $t = 0$, we have

$$y(0) = Ae^0 + \frac{b}{a} = A + \frac{b}{a}.$$

This implies that

$$A = y(0) - \frac{b}{a}.$$

Substituting A into the general solution yields

$$y(t) = \left[y(0) - \frac{b}{a}\right] e^{-at} + \frac{b}{a}, \quad a \neq 0. \tag{8.7}$$

Theorem 4: The definite solution to the non-homogeneous first-order linear differential equation $\frac{dy}{dt} + ay = b$ is $y(t) = \left[y(0) - \frac{b}{a}\right] e^{-at} + \frac{b}{a}$, where a is a constant coefficient with $a \neq 0$, and b is a constant term.

Example: Solve the equation $\frac{dy}{dt} + 4y = 2$ with the initial condition $y(0) = 100$.

From Theorem 4, we know that $y(t) = \left[y(0) - \frac{b}{a}\right] e^{-at} + \frac{b}{a}$. Here, $a = 4$ and $b = 2$. This implies

$$y(t) = [100 - 0.5]e^{-4t} + 0.5.$$

Thus, the definite solution to the differential equation under the initial condition $y(0) = 100$ is

$$y(t) = 99.5e^{-4t} + 0.5.$$

So far, we have assumed that the coefficient of the dependent variable, $a(t)$, is an arbitrary constant $a \neq 0$, and that the term $b(t)$ is either a constant b (in the non-homogeneous case) or zero (in the homogeneous case). We now consider the simpler case in which $a = 0$. In this case, the solution becomes $y(t) = bt + c$. To see this, we start from (8.5) and obtain

$$\frac{dy}{dt} = b.$$

Integrating both sides of the equation

$$\int \frac{dy}{dt} dt = \int bdt.$$

Thus, the general solution is

$$y(t) = bt + c,$$

where c is an arbitrary constant.

8.2.3 *Verification of the solution*

We have seen that the solutions to the reduced and the complete equations can be derived using integral calculus. Conversely, the validity of a solution can be verified by differentiation. The verification process involves two main steps. First, we differentiate the solution with respect to time t, which gives us $y'(t)$. Second, we substitute $y'(t)$ into the differential equation. More specifically, we substitute $y'(t)$ into (8.3) in the homogeneous case and $y'(t)$ into (8.5) in the non-homogeneous case. We then check whether each equation (reduced or complete) is consistent with its respective solution. Finally, we substitute $t = 0$ into the solution to verify whether the initial condition is satisfied.

Consider the non-homogeneous case ($a \neq 0$) where the complete equation is given by $\frac{dy}{dt} + ay = b$. Suppose we want to verify that the definite solution $y(t) = \left[y(0) - \frac{b}{a}\right] e^{-at} + \frac{b}{a}$ is valid. Differentiating the definite solution with respect to t gives us

$$\frac{dy}{dt} = \left[y(0) - \frac{b}{a}\right] e^{-at}(-a). \tag{8.8}$$

Substituting (8.8) and the definite solution given by (8.7) into the complete equation yields

$$-a\left[y(0) - \frac{b}{a}\right] e^{-at} + a\left[y(0) - \frac{b}{a}\right] e^{-at} + b = b.$$

This implies that the complete equation and its solution are consistent. Next, we check whether the solution satisfies the initial condition. Substituting $t = 0$ into the definite solution

$$\begin{aligned} y(0) &= \left[y(0) - \frac{b}{a}\right] e^{0} + \frac{b}{a}, \\ &= y(0) - \frac{b}{a} + \frac{b}{a}, \end{aligned}$$

which confirms the correctness of the solution to the complete equation.

8.3 Dynamics of Market Price

Consider the demand and supply functions for a particular commodity. Under the market-clearing condition, where demand equals supply, we can identify the equilibrium price P^*. Suppose the initial price $P(0)$ differs from the equilibrium price P^*. This assumption creates a need for dynamic analysis. Given sufficient time, will the price converge to the equilibrium level P^*? If so, we say that the equilibrium is *dynamically stable.*

To fix ideas, the supply function of a particular commodity is given by

$$Q_s = -c_s + \beta_s P$$

and the demand function is

$$Q_d = c_d - \beta_d P,$$

where β_s, β_d, c_s, $c_d > 0$. In equilibrium, the market clears, meaning that $Q_d = Q_s$, which results in the equilibrium price being

$$P^* = \frac{c_s + c_d}{\beta_s + \beta_d}. \tag{8.9}$$

Suppose that $P(0) \neq P^*$: the initial price differs from the equilibrium price. We ask whether, given sufficient time, the price will converge to the equilibrium level. That is, will $P(t) \to P^*$ as $t \to \infty$?

To answer this question, we begin by considering a specific pattern of price change. In particular, suppose that the change in price is proportional to the excess demand, $Q_d - Q_s$. This leads to the equation

$$\frac{dP}{dt} = A(Q_d - Q_s),$$

where $A > 0$ is a (constant) adjustment coefficient. Substituting Q_d for $c_d - \beta_d P$ and Q_s for $-c_s + \beta_s P$, we obtain

$$\frac{dP}{dt} = A(c_d - \beta_d P + c_s - \beta_s P).$$

This can be rewritten as

$$\frac{dP}{dt} + A(\beta_d + \beta_s)P = A(c_d + c_s),$$

which corresponds to a non-homogeneous first-order linear differential equation, similar to that shown in (8.5). In this case, the constant coefficient of the price is $A(\beta_d + \beta_s)$ and the constant term is $A(c_d + c_s)$. Recall that the definite solution of this equation takes the form

$$y(t) = y_c + y_p = \left[y(0) - \frac{b}{a}\right] e^{-at} + \frac{b}{a}.$$

Using this general solution, we can express the dynamics of price as follows:

$$P(t) = \left[P(0) - \frac{c_s + c_d}{\beta_s + \beta_d}\right] e^{-A(\beta_d+\beta_s)t} + \frac{c_s + c_d}{\beta_s + \beta_d}.$$

Substituting (8.9) allows us to answer the question of interest — whether $P(t)$ will converge to P^* as $t \to \infty$. We can write this as

$$P(t) = [P(0) - P^*]e^{-kt} + P^*, \tag{8.10}$$

where $k \equiv A(\beta_d + \beta_s) > 0$. From this expression, $[P(0) - P^*]e^{-kt}$ can be interpreted as the deviation of the time path from the equilibrium price level P^*. Rearranging Equation (8.10) yields

$$P(t) - P^* = [P(0) - P^*]e^{-kt}.$$

It follows that $P(t)$ will converge to P^* if $[P(0) - P^*]e^{-kt} \to 0$ as $t \to \infty$. Note that $e^{-kt} = 1/e^{kt}$. We know that $e^{kt} \to \infty$ as $t \to \infty$. Thus, $e^{-kt} \to 0$ as $t \to \infty$, suggesting that convergence is achieved. We conclude that the equilibrium is indeed *dynamically stable*. Further, we can interpret the convergence of $P(t)$ to P^* using simple diagrams, as shown in Figures 8.1(a) and 8.1(b). There are three possibilities.

1. **First case:** At time $t = 0$, the commodity is priced below the equilibrium level ($P(0) < P^*$). The resulting excess demand in the market will gradually increase the price until it reaches the equilibrium level. In this case, $P(t)$ approaches P^* from below, as illustrated in Figure 8.1(a).

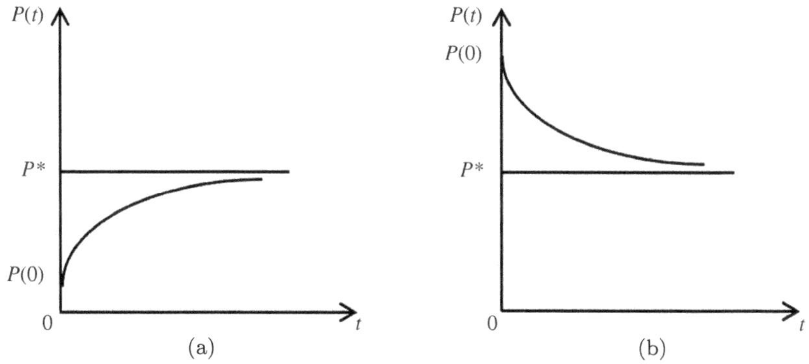

Figure 8.1

2. **Second case:** At time $t = 0$, the commodity is priced above the equilibrium level ($P(0) > P^*$). This leads to excess supply in the market which over time reduces the price to the equilibrium level. Thus, as shown in Figure 8.1(b), $P(t)$ approaches P^* from above.

3. **Third case:** It may be that at time $t = 0$, the commodity was priced exactly at the equilibrium level, so that $P(0) = P(t) = P^*$. In this case, the price always remains at the equilibrium level.

8.4 Variable Coefficient and Variable Term

In our previous analysis, we assumed that the coefficient and the term in Equation (8.5) are constants, that is $a(t) = a$ and $b(t) = b$. We now consider the more general case, where $a(t)$ and $b(t)$ are continuous functions of time t. In this case, we can express the first-order linear differential equation as

$$\frac{dy}{dt} + a(t)y = b(t).$$

Following the same approach as in the case of a constant coefficient and a constant term, we will first examine the homogeneous case, where $b(t) = 0$, before turning our attention to the non-homogeneous case.

8.4.1 *The homogeneous case*

In the special case where $b(t) = 0$, we have

$$\frac{dy}{dt} + a(t)y = 0. \tag{8.11}$$

Rearranging the terms gives us

$$\frac{dy}{dt} = -a(t)y.$$

Moving the y term to the left-hand side

$$\frac{1}{y}\frac{dy}{dt} = -a(t).$$

Integrating both sides, we obtain

$$\int \frac{1}{y}\frac{dy}{dt}dt = -\int a(t)dt.$$

This leads to

$$\ln y + c = -\int a(t)dt,$$

where $y > 0$. As we do not know the exact form of the function $a(t)$, we can rewrite the equation as follows:

$$\ln y = -c - \int a(t)dt.$$

Next, taking the antilog of $\ln y$

$$\begin{aligned} y(t) &= e^{-c}e^{-\int a(t)dt} \\ &= Ae^{-\int a(t)dt}, \end{aligned} \tag{8.12}$$

where $A \equiv e^{-c}$. Since the exact form of $a(t)$ is unknown, the solution derived here involves a general integral expression. However, with the aid of an initial condition, it is relatively straightforward to determine a specific solution. Notably, the general solutions in (8.4) and (8.12) are quite similar. In both cases, the coefficient of the variable y is integrated with respect to t (note that $\int adt = at$ plus a constant). By incorporating the constant into the term A, the only difference between (8.4) and (8.12) lies in the exponent of e: at in former case and $\int a(t)dt$ in the latter.

Example: Solve the equation $\frac{dy}{dt} + 5t^4 y = 0$ with the initial condition $y(0) = 100$.

We derive the solution to this differential equation by following the procedure outlined earlier. Rearranging the equation yields

$$\frac{dy}{dt} = -5t^4 y.$$

Moving the y term to the left-hand side and integrating both sides

$$\int \frac{1}{y}\frac{dy}{dt}dt = \int -5t^4 dt.$$

Calculating the integrals

$$\ln y + c_1 = -t^5 + c_2.$$

Letting $c \equiv c_2 - c_1$, we can simplify to

$$\ln y = c - t^5,$$

where $y > 0$. Taking the antilog of $\ln y$, we get

$$y(t) = Ae^{-t^5},$$

where $A \equiv e^c$. Substituting $t = 0$

$$y(0) = Ae^0 = A.$$

Thus, the definite solution is

$$y(t) = 100e^{-t^5}.$$

8.4.2 *The non-homogeneous case*

In the non-homogeneous case, the term $b(t)$ is non-zero. The first-order linear differential equation with a variable coefficient and a variable term is written as

$$\frac{dy}{dt} + a(t)y = b(t).$$

In the homogeneous case, where $b(t) = 0$, we have found the general solution to be

$$y(t) = Ae^{-\int a(t)dt}. \tag{8.13}$$

For the non-homogeneous case, where $b(t) \neq 0$, the general solution is given by

$$y(t) = e^{-\int a(t)dt}\left(A + \int b(t)e^{\int a(t)dt}dt\right). \tag{8.14}$$

Note that obtaining this solution is more complex and involves the use of *exact* differential equations, which will be explored in the next section.

Theorem 5: The general solution to the non-homogeneous first-order linear differential equation $\frac{dy}{dt} + a(t)y = b(t)$ is $y(t) = e^{-\int a(t)dt}(A + \int b(t)e^{\int a(t)dt}dt)$, where $a(t)$ is a variable coefficient, $b(t)$ is a variable term, and A is an arbitrary constant.

Given that we do not know the exact forms of the functions $a(t)$ and $b(t)$, we are unable to obtain a definite solution. However, when specific functional forms and an initial condition are available, it is possible to find a definite solution, as illustrated in the following example.

Example: Solve $\frac{dy}{dt} + 3t^2y = t^2$ with the initial condition $y(0) = \frac{2}{3}$.

Using Theorem 5, we can write the solution as

$$y(t) = e^{-\int 3t^2dt}\left(A + \int t^2e^{\int 3t^2dt}dt\right).$$

First, we calculate

$$\int 3t^2 dt = t^3 + k,$$

where k is arbitrary. Given that the constant A appears in the general solution, k can be subsumed under A. Substituting back this result, we have

$$y(t) = e^{-t^3}\left(A + \int t^2 e^{t^3} dt\right).$$

Next, we find the integral $\int t^2 e^{t^3} dt$. Using the substitution rule, we obtain[1]

$$\int t^2 e^{t^3} dt = \frac{1}{3}e^{t^3} + c.$$

Substituting this result into the expression for $y(t)$, we get

$$y(t) = e^{-t^3}\left(A + \frac{1}{3}e^{t^3}\right) = Ae^{-t^3} + \frac{1}{3}.$$

The next step is to definitize A using the initial condition

$$y(0) = A + \frac{1}{3} = \frac{2}{3}.$$

Solving for A

$$A = \frac{1}{3}.$$

Finally, substituting the value of A into the general solution yields

$$y(t) = \frac{1}{3}e^{-t^3} + \frac{1}{3}.$$

---

1 Letting $u = t^3$, we have $du = 3t^2 dt$, which implies that $dt = \frac{du}{3t^2}$. Substituting u and dt into the integral, we get: $\int t^2 e^{t^3} dt = \int t^2 e^u \frac{du}{3t^2} = \frac{1}{3}\int e^u du$. Calculating the integral yields: $\frac{1}{3}e^{t^3} + c$.

8.4.3 *Exact differential equations*

In this section, we derive the solution to the non-homogeneous first-order linear differential equation with a variable coefficient and a variable term. Suppose there exists a function $F(y, t)$ such that

$$dF(y,t) = \frac{\partial F(y,t)}{\partial y} dy + \frac{\partial F(y,t)}{\partial t} dt. \tag{8.15}$$

Setting this differential equal to zero, we obtain

$$\frac{\partial F(y,t)}{\partial y} dy + \frac{\partial F(y,t)}{\partial t} dt = 0. \tag{8.16}$$

Equation (8.16) is known as an *exact differential equation.* It is called exact because the left-hand side is exactly the total differential of the function $F(y, t)$.

Definition (Exact Differential Equation): Suppose there exists a function $F(y, t)$ such that

$$\frac{\partial F(y,t)}{\partial y} = M \quad \text{and} \quad \frac{\partial F(y,t)}{\partial t} = N.$$

The first-order linear differential equation of the form $Mdy + Ndt = 0$ is called exact.

To determine whether a differential equation is exact, we proceed as follows. First, we differentiate $\frac{\partial F(y,t)}{\partial y} = M$ with respect to t, and $\frac{\partial F(y,t)}{\partial t} = N$ with respect to y. This yields

$$\frac{\partial^2 F}{\partial y \partial t} = \frac{\partial M}{\partial t} \quad \text{and} \quad \frac{\partial^2 F}{\partial t \partial y} = \frac{\partial N}{\partial y}.$$

From Young's Theorem, we know that

$$\frac{\partial^2 F}{\partial y \partial t} = \frac{\partial^2 F}{\partial t \partial y}.$$

Hence, we have

$$\frac{\partial M}{\partial t} = \frac{\partial N}{\partial y}.$$

The following definition summarizes this result.

Definition (Exactness Test): A differential equation of the form

$$dF(y, t) = Mdy + Ndt = 0$$

is exact if and only if

$$\frac{\partial M}{\partial t} = \frac{\partial N}{\partial y},$$

where $M = \partial F / \partial y$ and $N = \partial F / \partial t$.

An application of the exactness test follows.

Example: Examine whether the function $F(y, t) = 2y^3 t + k$ corresponds to an exact differential equation.

Taking the total differential, we get

$$dF = (6y^2 t)dy + (2y^3)dt = 0,$$

where $6y^2 t = M$ and $2y^3 = N$. For this equation to be exact, it must satisfy the condition $\partial M / \partial t = \partial N / \partial y$. Differentiating M with respect to t and N with respect to y yields

$$\frac{\partial M}{\partial t} = 6y^2 = \frac{\partial N}{\partial y}.$$

Since these partial derivatives are equal, it follows that the function $F(y, t) = 2y^3 t + k$ corresponds to an exact differential equation.

Next, we discuss the solution method for an exact differential equation. As explained earlier, an exact differential equation takes the form

$$dF(y, t) = Mdy + Ndt = 0.$$

A preliminary result is given by

$$F(y,t) = \int M dy + \Psi(t).$$

The solution consists of the integral of M with respect to y, plus a new term, $\Psi(t)$, which is yet to be identified. Note that M is the partial derivative of $F(y,t)$ with respect to y, i.e., $\partial F(y,t)/\partial y$. Writing this preliminary result is the *first* step of the solution process. The *second* step involves taking the partial derivative of the preliminary result with respect to t. The *third* step requires finding the function $\Psi(t)$; this is done by integrating with respect to t the expression obtained in the second step. In the *final* step, we combine the results from the previous steps to obtain the solution to the differential equation. We now consider an example to clarify this process.

Example: Solve the exact differential equation $(1+3t^2)dy+(6ty-3t^2)dt = 0$.

We have $M = 1+3t^2$ and $N = 6ty - 3t^2$. First, the preliminary result is as follows:

$$F(y,t) = \int M dy + \Psi(t) = \int (1+3t^2)dy + \Psi(t).$$

Given that $M = 1 + 3t^2$ is integrated with respect to y (treating t as a constant), we obtain

$$F(y,t) = (1+3t^2)y + \Psi(t). \tag{8.17}$$

Note that the constant of integration has been incorporated into the expression for $\Psi(t)$. Then, differentiating (8.17) with respect to t, we get

$$\frac{\partial F(y,t)}{\partial t} = 6ty + \frac{\partial \Psi(t)}{\partial t}.$$

Recall that $\frac{\partial F(y,t)}{\partial t} = N$, with $N = 6ty - 3t^2$. Equating the expressions, we have

$$6ty - 3t^2 = 6ty + \frac{\partial \Psi(t)}{\partial t},$$

which implies

$$\frac{\partial \Psi(t)}{\partial t} = -3t^2.$$

Integrating both sides with respect to t, we obtain

$$\Psi(t) = -t^3 + c, \tag{8.18}$$

where c is an arbitrary constant. We then substitute (8.18) into (8.17) to find

$$F(y,t) = (1 + 3t^2)y - t^3 + c.$$

Because $dF(y,t) = 0$, the function $F(y,t)$ must be a constant; that is, $F(y,t) = A$. Substituting gives

$$A = (1 + 3t^2)y - t^3.$$

The constant c has been absorbed into A. Solving for y, we obtain

$$y(t) = \frac{A + t^3}{1 + 3t^2}.$$

Finally, letting $t = 0$ yields $y(0) = A$. Substituting this into the general solution leads to

$$y(t) = \frac{y(0) + t^3}{1 + 3t^2}.$$

8.4.4 *Integrating factor*

We examine a method that can be used to transform a differential equation that is not exact into an exact one. Specifically, an inexact differential equation can be made exact by multiplying every term of the equation by a particular common factor, known as the *integrating factor*. This enables us to apply the four-step solution procedure outlined earlier. Suppose we are given an inexact differential equation of the form

$$\frac{dy}{dt} + a(t)y = b(t).$$

Multiplying both sides of the equation by dt and rearranging the terms, we get

$$dy + [a(t)y - b(t)]dt = 0.$$

Next, we multiply the equation by the integrating factor $I(t)$ to obtain

$$I(t)dy + I(t)[a(t)y - b(t)]dt = 0. \tag{8.19}$$

We know that an exact differential equation takes the form $Mdy + Ndt = 0$, with $M = I(t)$ and $N = I(t)[a(t)y - b(t)]$ in the present case. For this equation to be exact, we require that $\partial M/\partial t = \partial N/\partial y$, which implies

$$\frac{dI(t)}{dt} = I(t)a(t).$$

Dividing both sides by $I(t)$ gives

$$\frac{dI(t)/dt}{I(t)} = a(t),$$

with the left-hand side representing the growth rate of $I(t)$. Note that the integrating factor takes the form

$$I(t) = e^{\int a(t)dt}.$$

This is true given that

$$\frac{dI(t)}{dt} = e^{\int a(t)dt}\left(\int a(t)dt\right)' = e^{\int a(t)dt}a(t).$$

The following definition summarizes this result.

Definition (Integrating Factor): The integrating factor $I(t)$ is a common factor that transforms an inexact differential equation of the form

$$\frac{dy}{dt} + a(t)y = b(t)$$

into an exact differential equation. It does so by multiplying every term of the equation by $I(t)$, where $I(t)$ is defined as

$$I(t) = e^{\int a(t)dt}.$$

8.4.5 *Applying the four-step solution procedure*

We have already introduced a method based on the use of the integrating factor. This method enables us to solve any first-order linear differential equation by transforming it into an exact differential equation. The general solution to the non-homogeneous case with a variable coefficient and a variable term is given by

$$y(t) = e^{-\int a(t)dt}\left(A + \int b(t)e^{\int a(t)dt}dt\right).$$

To obtain this solution, we first substitute the integrating factor $I(t) = e^{\int a(t)dt}$ into (8.19), which yields

$$e^{\int a(t)dt}dy + e^{\int a(t)dt}[a(t)y - b(t)]dt = 0.$$

The exact differential equation can then be written as

$$dF(y,t) = e^{\int a(t)dt}dy + e^{\int a(t)dt}[a(t)y - b(t)]dt = 0,$$

where $e^{\int a(t)dt} = M$ and $e^{\int a(t)dt}[a(t)y - b(t)] = N$. We can now apply the four-step procedure to solve this equation, starting with the preliminary result

$$F(y,t) = \int M dy + \Psi(t) = \int e^{\int a(t)dt} dy + \Psi(t)$$

or, equivalently,

$$F(y,t) = e^{\int a(t)dt} \int dy + \Psi(t) = ye^{\int a(t)dt} + \Psi(t). \tag{8.20}$$

The constant of integration has been merged with $\Psi(t)$. Differentiating (8.20) with respect to t gives us

$$\frac{\partial F(y,t)}{\partial t} = ye^{\int a(t)dt} a(t) + \frac{\partial \Psi(t)}{\partial t}.$$

We also know that $\partial F(y,t)/\partial t = N$ and $N = e^{\int a(t)dt}[a(t)y - b(t)]$. It follows that

$$e^{\int a(t)dt} a(t)y + \frac{\partial \Psi(t)}{\partial t} = e^{\int a(t)dt}[a(t)y - b(t)].$$

Solving for $\partial \Psi(t)/\partial t$ yields

$$\frac{\partial \Psi(t)}{\partial t} = -b(t)e^{\int a(t)dt}.$$

To find $\Psi(t)$, we integrate both sides of this equation with respect to t, which gives

$$\Psi(t) = -\int b(t)e^{\int a(t)dt} dt. \tag{8.21}$$

We then substitute (8.21) into (8.20) to obtain

$$F(y,t) = ye^{\int a(t)dt} - \int b(t)e^{\int a(t)dt} dt.$$

Recall that $F(y, t) = A$. Thus

$$A = ye^{\int a(t)dt} - \int b(t)e^{\int a(t)dt}dt.$$

Finally, solving for y gives us the desired result

$$y(t) = e^{-\int a(t)dt}\left(A + \int b(t)e^{\int a(t)dt}dt\right). \tag{8.22}$$

Example: Solve the differential equation $\frac{dy}{dt} + 2ty = 2t$.

We know that the solution to a first-order linear differential equation with a variable coefficient and a variable term is given by (8.22). Recall also Theorem 5 (the proof of which is based on the concept of an exact differential equation). This implies

$$y(t) = e^{-\int 2tdt}\left(A + \int 2te^{\int 2tdt}dt\right).$$

Calculating the integral $\int 2tdt$, we get

$$y(t) = e^{-t^2}\left(A + \int 2te^{t^2}dt\right).$$

We apply the substitution rule to find the integral $\int 2te^{t^2}dt$. Thus, we obtain

$$y(t) = e^{-t^2}(A + e^{t^2}).$$

We can express the solution as

$$y(t) = Ae^{-t^2} + 1.$$

To definitize A, we use the initial condition. Setting $t = 0$ yields

$$y(0) = A + 1.$$

Thus,

$$A = y(0) - 1.$$

The definite solution is then

$$y(t) = [y(0) - 1]e^{-t^2} + 1.$$

8.5 Further Exercises and Applications

(8.1) Suppose that a commodity in a particular market follows the price change pattern

$$\frac{dP}{dt} = 1.2(Q_d - Q_s),$$

where the demand and supply functions are given by

$$Q_d = 500 - 1.5P,$$

$$Q_s = -300 + P.$$

(i) Assuming the market clears, what is equilibrium price level P^*?

(ii) Is the equilibrium dynamically stable?

(iii) If $P(0) = 500$, what is the nature of the time path of the price?

Solution:

(i) Letting $Q_d = Q_s$, or directly using Equation (8.9), we get

$$P^* = \frac{300 + 500}{1 + 1.5} = 320.$$

(ii) From (8.10), we have

$$P(t) = [P(0) - P^*]e^{-kt} + P^*,$$

where $k \equiv A(\beta_d + \beta_s) = 1.2(1.5 + 1) = 3$ and $P^* = 320$. This can be rewritten as

$$P(t) - P^* = [P(0) - P^*]e^{-kt}.$$

Thus, $P(t)$ will converge to P^* if $[P(0) - P^*]e^{-kt} \to 0$ as $t \to \infty$. Given that $e^{-kt} \to 0$ as $t \to \infty$, convergence is achieved. The equilibrium is therefore dynamically stable.

(iii) Given that $P(0) = 500 > P^*$, $P(t)$ will approach P^* from above.

(8.2) Verify that $y(t) = 100e^{-t^5}$ is the solution to the differential equation $\frac{dy}{dt} + 5t^4y = 0$ with the initial condition $y(0) = 100$.

Solution:

Differentiating the solution with respect to t yields

$$\frac{dy}{dt} = -500t^4e^{-t^5}.$$

Substituting this into the differential equation, we obtain

$$\frac{dy}{dt} + 5t^4y = -500t^4e^{-t^5} + 5t^4(100e^{-t^5}) = 0.$$

Thus, the solution satisfies the differential equation. Finally, we check the initial condition

$$y(0) = 100e^0 = 100.$$

(8.3) Examine whether the differential equation $3tydy + y^2dt = 0$ is exact.

Solution:

We have $3ty = M$ and $y^2 = N$. Differentiating M with respect to t and N with respect to y gives

$$\frac{\partial M}{\partial t} = 3y \quad \text{and} \quad \frac{\partial N}{\partial y} = 2y.$$

Because $\partial M/\partial t \neq \partial N/\partial y$, the differential equation $3tydy + y^2dt = 0$ is not exact.

(8.4) Solve $\frac{dy}{dt} + 4ty = 6t$ with the initial condition $y(0) = 5/2$.

Solution:

Using Theorem 5, we can write the solution as

$$\begin{aligned} y(t) &= e^{-\int 4tdt}\left(A + \int 6t\, e^{\int 4tdt} dt\right) \\ &= e^{-2t^2}\left(A + \int 6t\, e^{2t^2} dt\right). \end{aligned}$$

We apply the substitution rule to find the integral $\int 6t\, e^{2t^2} dt$. Let $2t^2 = u$, so that $4tdt = du$, or equivalently, $dt = du/4t$. Thus,

$$\int 6t\, e^{2t^2} dt = \int 6t\, e^u \frac{du}{4t}.$$

This integral simplifies to

$$\frac{3}{2}\int e^u du = \frac{3}{2}e^u + c = \frac{3}{2}e^{2t^2} + c.$$

It follows that

$$y(t) = Ae^{-2t^2} + \frac{3}{2},$$

where the constant c has been absorbed into A. Next, we definitize the arbitrary constant A. Using the initial condition $y(0) = 5/2$, we have

$$y(0) = A + \frac{3}{2} = \frac{5}{2}.$$

Thus, $A = 1$. Finally, substituting $A = 1$ into the general solution yields

$$y(t) = e^{-2t^2} + \frac{3}{2}.$$

The correctness of the solution can be verified using the two-step procedure outlined in Section 8.2.3.

Further Reading

Arrow, K. J. & Hahn, F. H. (1971). *General Competitive Analysis.* San Francisco, Holden-Day.

Chiang, A. C. & Wainwright, K. (2005). *Fundamental Methods of Mathematical Economics.* Boston, McGraw-Hill.

Dawkins, P. (2007). Paul's Online Math Notes. Retrieved September 2016, from Differential Equations: https://tutorial.math.lamar.edu/.

Hirsch, M. W., Smale, S., & Devaney, R. L. (2004). *Differential Equations, Dynamical Systems, and an Introduction to Chaos.* Waltham, Academic Press.

Luderer, B., Nollau, V., & Vetters, K. (2009). *Mathematical Formulas for Economists.* Berlin, Springer Science & Business Media.

Simon, C. P. & Blume, L. (1994). *Mathematics for Economists.* New York, Norton.

Sydsaeter, K., Hammond, P., Seierstad, A. & Strom, A. (2008). *Further Mathematics for Economic Analysis* (second edition). Harlow, Pearson.

Trench, W. F. (2001). *Elementary Differential Equations.* Pacific Grove, Brooks/Cole Thomson Learning.

CHAPTER 9

RESEARCH APPLICATIONS

Learning Objectives

After completing this chapter, students will be able to:

- Understand how the techniques of partial differentiation, total differentiation, and unconstrained optimization can be used in research applications.
- Appreciate the applications of mathematics in both theoretical and empirical research in economics.

We have seen that the techniques of differentiation and optimization are useful for analyzing the decisions of economic agents, such as consumers and firms. In this chapter, we will explore how these techniques can be applied in two settings from my own research. The first example comes from the field of industrial organization, which uses concepts from game theory to study strategic interactions between agents. These agents can be thought of as players in a game that involves one or more stages of strategic interaction. A player's optimal strategy at any stage depends on the optimal strategies of the other players. As we will see, the study of such interactions relies primarily on two techniques: differentiation and optimization.

The second example comes from a different area of research: the economics of well-being. In recent years, economists and other social scientists are increasingly relying on measures of subjective well-being as proxies for individual utility or welfare. I examine the link between subjective well-being and physical health, and discuss how this link can be explained by "third" variables, known as mediators. The central hypothesis is that individuals' well-being affects their physical health not only directly but also indirectly. The total derivatives discussed in Chapter 2 capture all possible channels — both direct and indirect — through which the influence of an independent variable of interest is transmitted to the dependent variable. This observation is useful for setting up an empirical test of the hypothesis that the effects of well-being on physical health are mediated by different types of health investments.

The first example is theoretical in nature, while the second is empirical. The choice of both these examples is deliberate and aims to demonstrate that mathematics has immediate applications in many fields of economics. Over the last 20 years of conducting research, I have come to the conclusion that both methods — theoretical analysis and empirical investigation — complement each other: empirical tests provide direction to theorists by identifying suitable models, while theoretical predictions help set the agenda for empirical work.

9.1 Example: R&D Subsidies, Spillovers, and Privatization

Over the last few decades, several countries around the world have undertaken extensive privatization programs. Despite the popularity of privatization, economists have often argued in favor of maintaining the presence of public firms in different market environments.[1] Our first example addresses this issue and comes from the paper titled *R&D Subsidies, Spillovers and Privatization in Mixed Markets*, which appeared in the *Southern Economic Journal* (see Gil-Moltó *et al.*, 2011).[2] This chapter compares a mixed market setting with a private one: in the former, a state-owned or public firm competes with a private firm, while in the latter, both firms are private.

The chapter's objective is two-fold. First, it highlights the importance of R&D subsidies for the R&D investments of both public and private firms. Second, it compares the performance of a mixed market and a private market in cost-reducing investment, and provides some guidelines regarding the privatization of the public firm. The aim is to compute the equilibrium outcomes in the two market settings — the mixed market and the private market — using the techniques of differentiation and optimization that were studied earlier.

9.1.1 *The model*

9.1.1.1 *Preliminaries*

Consider a simple market setting consisting of two firms. In a mixed duopoly, one firm is public and the other is private. In a private duopoly, both firms are private. The main difference between a private and a public firm is that the former is assumed to maximize profit, whereas the latter maximizes social welfare. In the mixed duopoly, let the subscript 0 denote the public firm and the

---

1 A systematic discussion of public firms and their objectives is offered by Poyago-Theotoky (2024).

2 For more information, the reader can refer to Zikos (2007a, 2007b) and Kesavayuth and Zikos (2013). A related study examines a mixed oligopoly, where a public firm competes with n private firms, and compares it to a private oligopoly (see Gil-Moltó *et al.*, 2020).

subscript 1 denote the private firm. The (inverse) demand function is of the standard form

$$P(Q) = a - Q, \tag{9.1}$$

where $Q = q_i + q_j$ is the total output, with $i \neq j$ and $i, j \in \{0, 1\}$.

9.1.1.2 *Sequencing of moves*

To model the strategic interactions between the two firms, we consider a multi-stage game. The time structure of the game is as follows: in *stage one*, the government chooses the level of a subsidy (or tax, if negative) to R&D in order to maximize social welfare. In *stage two*, the firms simultaneously choose their R&D investments. In *stage three*, the firms choose their output quantities. The game is solved using backward induction.

9.1.1.3 *R&D investments and production costs*

One of the key features in this market is that the firms undertake R&D investments. The firms invest in cost-reducing R&D, also known as *process* R&D. The level of effective R&D is given by

$$X_i = x_i + \beta x_j, \tag{9.2}$$

where $i \neq j$ and $i, j \in \{0, 1\}$. X_i represents the total reduction in a firm's marginal cost due to R&D. It has two components: the firm's own R&D output, x_i, and the competitor's R&D output, x_j. The competitor's R&D output influences firm i via spillovers. The degree of spillovers is captured by the parameter β, with $0 \leq \beta \leq 1$, and is assumed to be exogenously given. This means that the level of β is influenced by factors outside the firms' control, such as the strength of the patent system.[3]

[3] A weaker patent system, for instance, suggests a relatively higher spillover rate β. In the extreme case where there is no patent protection at all, we have $\beta = 1$.

To study a mixed duopoly, one must avoid situations where the private firm is driven out of the market entirely. To that end, a standard assumption in the literature is employed: the existence of diminishing returns to scale. This is introduced by adding a quadratic term related to production in the firms' total cost functions. Accordingly, firm i's cost function depends on its output, q_i, as well as the level of effective R&D, X_i. That is

$$C_i(q_i, X_i) = (c - X_i)q_i + q_i^2, \tag{9.3}$$

where $i \in \{0, 1\}$ and $a > c > 0$. Differentiating (9.3) with respect to q_i gives us the marginal cost of production

$$mc_i = \partial C_i / \partial q_i = (c - X_i) + 2q_i. \tag{9.4}$$

It is interesting to observe how the level of effective R&D affects firm i's marginal cost. X_i affects the intercept of the marginal cost. In other words, X_i shifts the marginal cost curve downwards. This idea is in line with the seminal work of d' Aspremont and Jacquemin (1988),[4] which appeared in the prestigious *American Economic Review* and stimulated a large literature on R&D investments in different market settings (see e.g., Kamien *et al.*, 1992; Cassiman and Veugelers, 2002; Eckel and Neary, 2010; Becker, 2015; López and Vives, 2019; Gil-Moltó *et al.*, 2020; Sovinsky, 2022).

The R&D cost function is given by $\Gamma(x_i) = \gamma x_i^2$, where $\gamma > 0$. This reflects diminishing returns to the level of R&D investment, x_i. For tractability, we set $\gamma = 1$, which ensures non-negativity of all variables. Hence, spending x_i^2 on R&D implies two things. First, a firm can lower its costs by x_i as a result of its own research effort. Second, a firm can further lower its costs by βx_j as it is able to appropriate part of the rival firm's research effort via spillovers.

[4] At the time of writing, this influential paper had received more than 3,834 citations.

In addition, each firm receives a government subsidy. This subsidy is paid per unit of R&D output, so that $S(x_i) = sx_i$.

9.1.1.4 *Profit functions and social welfare*

The profit function of the private firm is written as

$$\pi_i = P(Q)q_i - C_i(q_i, X_i) - \Gamma(x_i) + S(x_i). \tag{9.5}$$

The public firm, unlike the private one, is assumed to maximize social welfare. This consists of three components: consumer surplus (CS), producer surplus (PS), and R&D subsidies

$$\mathrm{SW} = \underbrace{\frac{1}{2}Q^2}_{\text{CS}} + \underbrace{(\pi_i + \pi_j)}_{\text{PS}} - \underbrace{s(x_i + x_j)}_{\text{Subsidy}}. \tag{9.6}$$

Note that in (9.6), the subsidy enters the profit functions of both firms, so it cancels out when aggregating. This means that the subsidy has no direct impact on social welfare, and hence on the objective function of the public firm. However, the subsidy exerts an indirect impact on the public firm, as it affects the private firm's R&D choice. Thus, the role of an R&D subsidy is two-fold. First, given that the public firm is less efficient than the private one, the subsidy helps improve the distribution of production costs between the firms. In other words, the subsidy has a cost-shifting effect. Second, the subsidy stimulates R&D spending and thereby addresses the fact that R&D investment is less than the social optimum.

9.1.2 *A private duopoly market*

We begin our analysis with the case in which both firms are private.

9.1.2.1 *Output decisions*

In the final stage of the game, both firms choose their output levels to maximize their profits. The first-order condition (foc, henceforth) of this maximization problem is[5]

$$(a - c) - 4q_i - q_j + (x_i + \beta x_j) = 0. \tag{9.7}$$

The second-order condition (soc, henceforth) is $-4 < 0$. The soc is satisfied, hence the focs are necessary and sufficient for an interior optimum. Solving the system of the focs, we obtain the Cournot-Nash equilibrium quantities

$$q_i^p(x_i, x_j) = \frac{3(a-c) + (4-\beta)x_i + (4\beta - 1)x_j}{15}. \tag{9.8}$$

Substituting (9.8) into the firms' profit functions allows us to express profits in terms of R&D investments and the subsidy.

9.1.2.2 *R&D investment decisions*

In stage two, the firms choose their R&D levels to maximize their profits. The focs are given by

$$\begin{aligned} &12(4-\beta)(a-c) - 2[193 + 2\beta(8-\beta)]x_i \\ &- 4(4-\beta)(1-4\beta)x_j + 225s = 0. \end{aligned} \tag{9.9}$$

The soc for firm i is $-2[193 + 2\beta(8-\beta)] < 0$. The focs are both necessary and sufficient for an interior optimum. Solving the foc of each firm i with respect to x_i gives us the R&D best-response functions,

$$r_i^p(x_j) = \frac{12(4-\beta)(a-c) - 4(4-\beta)(1-4\beta)x_j + 225s}{2[193 + 2\beta(8-\beta)]}. \tag{9.10}$$

Solving the system of the R&D best-response functions leads to the equilibrium R&D levels

$$x_i^p(s) = \frac{4(4-\beta)(a-c) + 75s}{2[67 - 2\beta(3-\beta)]}, \tag{9.11}$$

5 The computations were performed using the software Mathematica.

where $i \in \{0, 1\}$. Note that the subsidy has a positive effect on each private firm's R&D investment.

9.1.2.3 *R&D subsidy decision*

Substituting (9.11) into (9.8) allows us to express equilibrium output as a function of the subsidy s

$$q_i^p(s) = \frac{15[2(a-c)+s(1+\beta)]}{2[67-2\beta(3-\beta)]}. \tag{9.12}$$

Next, we substitute the R&D levels and output quantities into the social welfare function. Differentiating the resulting expression with respect to s gives us

$$\frac{300(a-c)(1+11\beta)-450s(22-6\beta-3\beta^2)}{2[67-2\beta(3-\beta)]^2} = 0. \tag{9.13}$$

The corresponding soc is $-225(22-6\beta-3\beta^2)/[67-2\beta(3-\beta)]^2 < 0$. Solving the foc in (9.13) with respect to the choice variable s leads to

$$s^p = \frac{2(1+11\beta)(a-c)}{3[22-3\beta(2+\beta)]}. \tag{9.14}$$

From (9.14), we can see that s^p is positive. Further, differentiating s^p with respect to β yields

$$\frac{\partial s^p}{\partial \beta} = \frac{2(a-c)(248+6\beta+33\beta^2)}{3[22-3\beta(2+\beta)]^2} > 0. \tag{9.15}$$

We then substitute (9.14) into (9.11) and (9.12) to obtain the equilibrium solutions for R&D and output

$$x_i^p = \frac{3(1+\beta)(a-c)}{22-3\beta(2+\beta)}, \tag{9.16}$$

$$q_i^p = \frac{5(a-c)}{22-3\beta(2+\beta)}. \tag{9.17}$$

Substituting (9.14), (9.16), and (9.17) into (9.5) gives each firm's profit

$$\pi_i^p = \frac{[43 + \beta(6 + 13\beta)](a - c)^2}{[22 - 3\beta(2 + \beta)]^2}. \tag{9.18}$$

Finally, substituting into the expression for consumer surplus, $(1/2)Q^2$, as well as into the expression for social welfare (9.6), reveals the following equilibrium outcomes

$$\text{CS}^p = \frac{50(a - c)^2}{[22 - 3\beta(2 + \beta)]^2}, \tag{9.19}$$

$$\text{SW}^p = \frac{6(a - c)^2}{22 - 3\beta(2 + \beta)}. \tag{9.20}$$

9.1.3 *A mixed duopoly market*

9.1.3.1 *Output decisions*

In this section, we derive the equilibrium for a mixed duopoly market. Unlike the private duopoly, here a public firm competes against a private one. In the last stage of the game, each firm chooses its output quantity to maximize its objective function: the private firm maximizes profits, whereas the public firm maximizes welfare. Each firm thus solves its own optimization problem and, in doing so, takes the other firm's output quantity as given. The focs for the public and private firms, respectively, are

$$(a - c) - 3q_0 - q_1 + (x_0 + \beta x_1) = 0, \tag{9.21}$$

$$(a - c) - 4q_1 - q_0 + (x_1 + \beta x_0) = 0. \tag{9.22}$$

The soc for the public firm is $-3 < 0$, and for the private firm $-4 < 0$. It follows that the focs are both necessary and sufficient for an interior optimum. Solving the system of the focs, we obtain the Cournot–Nash equilibrium quantities

$$q_0^m(x_0, x_1) = \frac{3(a-c) + (4-\beta)x_0 + (4\beta - 1)x_1}{11}, \tag{9.23}$$

$$q_1^m(x_0, x_1) = \frac{2(a-c) + (3\beta - 1)x_0 + (3-\beta)x_1}{11}. \tag{9.24}$$

As expected, each firm's R&D has a larger impact on its own output than on the rival firm's output; that is, $4 - \beta \geq 4\beta - 1$ and $3 - \beta \geq 3\beta - 1$.[6] Substituting the equilibrium quantities into the private firm's profit function (9.5) and the social welfare function (9.6) allows us to proceed to the second stage of the game, where firms choose their R&D levels.

9.1.3.2 *R&D investment decisions*

In the second stage, each firm chooses its R&D output (cost reduction) to maximize its objective function, taking the other firm's R&D output as given. The focs for this problem are

$$\begin{aligned} &(31 + 28\beta)(a - c) - [14 - \beta(87 - 14\beta)]x_1 \\ &\quad - [197 + 14\beta(2 - 3\beta)]x_0 = 0, \end{aligned} \tag{9.25}$$

$$\begin{aligned} &8(3 - \beta)(a - c) - 4(3 - \beta)(1 - 3\beta)x_0 \\ &\quad - [206 + 4\beta(6 - \beta)]x_1 + 121s = 0. \end{aligned} \tag{9.26}$$

The corresponding socs are $-(197 + 14\beta(2 - 3\beta)) < 0$ and $-(206 + 4\beta(6 - \beta)) < 0$ for the public firm and for the private firm, respectively. Solving (9.25) with respect to x_0 and (9.26) with respect to

[6] An exception arises in the case of perfect spillovers ($\beta = 1$). This reflects the absence of patent protection, meaning that each firm can fully appropriate the other firm's R&D output.

x_1 gives us the R&D best-response functions

$$r_0(x_1) = \frac{(31 + 28\beta)(a - c) - [14 - \beta(87 - 14\beta)]x_1}{197 + 14\beta(2 - 3\beta)}, \tag{9.27}$$

$$r_1(x_0) = \frac{8(3 - \beta)(a - c) - 4(3 - \beta)(1 - 3\beta)x_0 + 121s}{206 + 4\beta(6 - \beta)}. \tag{9.28}$$

Solving the system of (9.27) and (9.28) leads to the R&D outputs

$$x_0^m(s) = \frac{2[25 + 2\beta(18 - \beta)](a - c) - s[14 - \beta(87 - 14\beta)]}{2[167 + 2\beta(25 - \beta)(1 - \beta)]}, \tag{9.29}$$

$$x_1^m(s) = \frac{4(9 - \beta^2)(a - c) + s[197 + 14\beta(2 - 3\beta)]}{2[167 + 2\beta(25 - \beta)(1 - \beta)]}. \tag{9.30}$$

We then substitute the R&D outputs into (9.23) and (9.24), which allows us to express the equilibrium quantities as functions of the subsidy s

$$q_0^m(s) = \frac{2[53 + \beta(31 - 18\beta)](a - c) + s[-23 + \beta(102 + \beta - 14\beta^2)]}{2[167 + 2\beta(25 - \beta)(1 - \beta)]}, \tag{9.31}$$

$$q_1^m(s) = \frac{11[2(3 + \beta)(a - c) + s(5 - \beta(2 - \beta))]}{2[167 + 2\beta(25 - \beta)(1 - \beta)]}. \tag{9.32}$$

9.1.3.3 *R&D subsidy decision*

We now turn to the first stage of the game to derive the optimal R&D subsidy. The government's optimization problem is to choose the value of the subsidy that maximizes social welfare. However, before solving this problem, we need to perform an additional substitution. Specifically, we substitute the R&D levels and output quantities into the social welfare function. After making these substitutions, we differentiate the resulting expression with respect to the subsidy s. This gives us the foc

$$\frac{\begin{array}{c}(197+28\beta-42\beta^2)(2(a-c)(3+32\beta+17\beta^2-9\beta^3)\\ -s(162+56\beta-101\beta^2+7\beta^4))\end{array}}{2(167+50\beta-52\beta^2+2\beta^3)^2}=0. \quad (9.33)$$

The soc is $-(197+28\beta-42\beta^2)(162+56\beta-101\beta^2+7\beta^4)/2(167+50\beta-52\beta^2+2\beta^3)^2<0$. Solving the foc yields the equilibrium R&D subsidy

$$s^m=\frac{2[3+\beta(32+17\beta-9\beta^2)](a-c)}{162+\beta[56-\beta(101-7\beta^2)]}. \quad (9.34)$$

Next, we substitute (9.34) into (9.29) and (9.30) to obtain the equilibrium R&D levels

$$x_0^m=\frac{[24+7\beta(5+\beta(1-\beta))](a-c)}{162+\beta[56-\beta(101-7\beta^2)]}, \quad (9.35)$$

$$x_1^m=\frac{[21+\beta(38+7\beta(1-\beta))](a-c)}{162+\beta[56-\beta(101-7\beta^2)]}. \quad (9.36)$$

Similarly, using (9.34) together with (9.31) and (9.32), we obtain the equilibrium output levels

$$q_0^m=\frac{3[17+5\beta(2-\beta)](a-c)}{162+\beta[56-\beta(101-7\beta^2)]}, \quad (9.37)$$

$$q_1^m=\frac{11(3-\beta)(1+\beta)(a-c)}{162+\beta[56-\beta(101-7\beta^2)]}. \quad (9.38)$$

Substituting (9.34), (9.35), (9.36), (9.37), and (9.38) into (9.5) gives us the equilibrium profits

$$\pi_0^m=\frac{\begin{array}{c}[2169+\beta(3126+907\beta+110\beta^2-174\beta^3\\ -266\beta^4+77\beta^5)](a-c)^2\end{array}}{[162+\beta(56-\beta(101-7\beta^2))]^2}, \quad (9.39)$$

$$\pi_1^m=\frac{\begin{array}{c}[1863+\beta(2880+966\beta+114\beta^2-169\beta^3\\ -266\beta^4+77\beta^5)](a-c)^2\end{array}}{[162+\beta(56-\beta(101-7\beta^2))]^2}. \quad (9.40)$$

Finally, substituting into the expressions for consumer surplus and social welfare reveals the following equilibrium outcomes:

$$\mathrm{CS}^m = \frac{2[42 + 13\beta(2-\beta)]^2(a-c)^2}{[162 + \beta(56 - \beta(101 - 7\beta^2))]^2}, \tag{9.41}$$

$$\mathrm{SW}^m = \frac{[45 + 14\beta(2-\beta)](a-c)^2}{162 + \beta[56 - \beta(101 - 7\beta^2)]}. \tag{9.42}$$

9.1.4 *Main results*

Using the equilibrium outcomes from Sections 9.1.2 and 9.1.3, we can compare several aspects of the two market settings: R&D subsidies, R&D output, profits, and social welfare. This simple comparative static analysis serves the purpose of capturing the effects of privatization. As such, it generates a number of original conclusions that have been referenced frequently.[7]

The analysis of the equilibrium outcomes is straightforward and, in many cases, is based on simple algebra — specifically, calculating the difference between two equilibrium quantities and determining the sign of the resulting mathematical expression. For example, comparing the welfare levels in the private and mixed market settings, as given in (9.20) and (9.42), suggests that privatization reduces welfare: $\mathrm{SW}^p - \mathrm{SW}^m < 0$ for all $\beta \in [0, 1]$. Another interesting result concerns the optimal R&D subsidy. We find that the optimal subsidy is positive and increases with the degree of spillovers. This is true in both the private and mixed duopoly settings, although the subsidy is lower in the private duopoly than in the mixed one.

[7] At the time of writing this chapter, the paper by Gil-Moltó *et al.* (2011) had been cited over 125 times.

To show that the optimal R&D subsidy in the mixed duopoly is always positive and increases with the rate of spillovers, we proceed as follows. Differentiating Equation (9.34) with respect to β, we obtain

$$\frac{ds^m}{d\beta} = \frac{B(a-c)}{C^2},$$

where $B \equiv 2(5016 + 6114\beta - 190\beta^2 - 1092\beta^3 + 237\beta^4 - 238\beta^5 + 63\beta^6 > 0$ and $C \equiv 162 + \beta[56 - \beta(101 - 7\beta^2)] > 0$ for all $\beta \in [0, 1]$. Given that $(a - c) > 0$, this implies that $ds^m/d\beta > 0$. Next, we evaluate the optimal R&D subsidy when the spillover rate is 0. Substituting $\beta = 0$ into (9.34) gives $6(a - c)/162 > 0$. By continuity, we have that $s^m > 0$ for all β. This completes the proof that the subsidy is positive and increasing in β.

The findings presented here, together with those in Gil-Moltó *et al.* (2011), can be valuable in informing public policies. First, policymakers should adjust the optimal level of the R&D subsidy based on the degree of spillovers. Specifically, firms should receive a higher subsidy as the rate of spillovers increases. Second, there is a welfare-related argument against favoring the privatization of the public firm. This reasoning supports the case for caution regarding the widespread adoption of privatization programs (see Radić *et al.*, 2021, for a review).

These policy implications have been derived within a duopoly model. Therefore, care should be taken when generalizing them to markets with a larger number of private and public firms. The main conclusions of the chapter were examined in further research conducted with my colleagues Maria-Jose Gil-Moltó, Joanna Poyago-Theotoky and Jose Rodrigues-Neto (see Gil-Moltó *et al.*, 2020). This work drew on recent developments in game theory, specifically aggregative game techniques, to compare the equilibrium outcomes in private and mixed oligopoly markets.[8]

9.2 Example: Subjective Well-Being and Physical Health

Economists are increasingly interested in the study of subjective well-being. The 2009 Commission on the Measurement of Economic Performance and Social Progress, initiated by the French government and led by Joseph Stiglitz, argued that traditional economic indicators like GDP are inadequate for assessing social progress. It emphasized the need to prioritize people's reported well-being (Stiglitz *et al.*, 2010). Given the substantial spending on welfare in many developed countries,[9] it is important to examine whether this spending could have positive effects on objective outcomes such as physical health.

This study seeks to explore this issue, based on joint work with my colleagues Dusanee Kesavayuth and Prompong Shangkhum (see Kesavayuth *et al.*, 2022a). Unlike the theoretical study in Section 9.1, which used differentiation, optimization, and game theory techniques, the current study is empirical. It examines the relationship between subjective well-being and physical health, focusing on how this link might be mediated by "third" variables. To do this, I apply total derivatives from Chapter 2 to examine all possible

8 Two closely related papers are Zikos (2010) and Kesavayuth and Zikos (2013). The former investigates the formation of R&D collaboration networks in a mixed oligopoly, while the latter explores the relative welfare effects of R&D and output subsidies.

9 For more information, see the "Mental Health and Well-Being Budget 2021–22" in Australia.

channels — both direct and indirect — through which an independent variable of interest affects the dependent variable. The main goal is to empirically test the hypothesis that the effects of well-being on physical health are mediated by various types of health investments.

Earlier studies suggest that people's health status influences how they report their well-being. While this finding is not new, recent empirical evidence also points to the reverse possibility: well-being itself may help protect physical health. For instance, individuals with higher levels of well-being tend to have lower blood pressure (Blanchflower and Oswald, 2008), perform better in daily activities (Ohrnberger *et al.*, 2017), experience fewer chronic conditions and functional impairments (Ryff *et al.*, 2015), have better immune function (Barak, 2006), and may live longer (Steptoe *et al.*, 2015; O'Connor and Graham, 2019). The emerging evidence is clear: positive well-being may play an important role in health and longevity.

What explains the protective role of well-being in physical health? Steptoe *et al.* (2015) suggest that lifestyle factors, such as physical activity, may help explain this relationship. Regular physical activity is linked to numerous health benefits, including improved cardiovascular health, muscle strength, flexibility, and healthy body weight (Windle *et al.*, 2010). Furthermore, physical activity is associated with higher levels of well-being (Rasciute and Downward, 2010). While Steptoe *et al.* (2015) recognize that a deeper understanding of the behavioral pathways linking well-being to better physical health opens up intriguing possibilities, they do not formally test this hypothesis.

In this study, we aim to fill this research gap by developing a mediation framework to test whether two forms of human capital investments — lifestyle choices and social capital — act as pathways through which subjective well-being influences physical health. Both types of investments are important because they are critical inputs in health and highly relevant to welfare policies. Our objective is to quantify the direct effects of life satisfaction on physical health and the indirect, mediational pathways through lifestyle choices and social capital.

To preface our results, we find that individuals who are more satisfied with their life tend to have better physical health. This effect is largely explained by physical activity, smoking behavior, and social interaction. We also observe gender differences in these findings, with the share of the indirect effect in the total effect being about 14% for females, but much larger for males, at 23%.

These results contribute to several strands of related literature. The first is the economics literature on subjective well-being. While the role of well-being as an outcome variable has been extensively studied, there is a growing consensus that well-being is not only the result but also the cause of many behavioral and economic outcomes, including wages, employment, healthy behaviors, and longevity (e.g., Boehm *et al.*, 2012; Mishra and Smyth, 2014; Kesavayuth and Zikos, 2018; O'Connor and Graham, 2019). We contribute to this body of research by examining whether individuals' well-being is linked to their physical health.

A second set of studies to which we contribute are those on the determinants of physical health. Most earlier studies have not explored the link between well-being and physical health. While a few studies have examined the impact of mental health on physical health (e.g., Rowan *et al.*, 2005; Surtees *et al.*, 2008; Ohrnberger *et al.*, 2017; Kesavayuth *et al.*, 2022b; Yang and Zikos, 2022), we extend this literature by investigating whether life satisfaction influences physical health and, if so, what factors might explain this relationship.

A third set of studies to which we contribute are those using mediation analysis to understand the relationship between two variables through the inclusion of "third" variables, known as mediators. Some studies offer methodological contributions (e.g., Vanderweele, 2015; Vanderweele and Tchetgen Tchetgen, 2017), while others apply these techniques in various contexts (e.g., Ohrnberger *et al.*, 2017; Magnani and Zhu, 2018; Tran *et al.*, 2021; Kesavayuth *et al.*, 2020, 2021; Awaworyi Churchill and Smyth, 2021). Our study provides some of the first empirical evidence on the direct and indirect effects of well-being on physical health within a mediation framework. In addition to their empirical significance, our findings may provide valuable insights for health professionals and policymakers in designing and targeting interventions to improve people's health.

9.2.1 *Data and description of the main variables*

The data source for this analysis is the Household Income and Labour Dynamics of Australia (HILDA) Survey, a longitudinal study of a nationally representative sample of Australian households. We analyze waves 11–18 of the HILDA Survey, covering the period 2011–2018. Our analytical sample includes respondents aged 15–80, corresponding to an unbalanced panel of 75,043 observations from 17,431 individuals.

Our dependent variable is physical health, derived from the 36-item Short Form Health Survey (SF-36). Of the 36 items, 21 pertain to physical health, which is measured across four dimensions: physical functioning, role-physical, bodily pain, and general health. The HILDA Survey provides each dimension on a 0–100 scale, with higher values indicating better health. The Cronbach's alpha reliability statistic is slightly above 0.84, allowing us to generate a summary measure by averaging the scores of the four physical health dimensions for each observation. We also constructed an alternative physical health index using factor analysis in robustness checks, which led to qualitatively similar conclusions.

Our key independent variable, life satisfaction, is one of the most widely used indicators of subjective well-being. In the HILDA Survey, respondents were asked to rate their overall life satisfaction, with answers ranging from 0 (totally dissatisfied) to 10 (totally satisfied). This measure reflects a cognitive or evaluative assessment of the respondent's life as a whole (Powdthavee, 2010, 2015). Life satisfaction has been validated and shown to be a good proxy for subjective well-being (Pavot and Diener, 1993). Given that life satisfaction is coded on a 0 to 10 scale, we divided physical health by 10 so that both variables are on the same scale. The summary statistics and description of all the variables included in the analyses appear in Table 9.1.

9.2.2 *Empirical model*

Diener *et al.* (2017) suggest that mediation analysis should account for the sequencing of events. Thus, instead of using contemporaneous values of the dependent and explanatory variables, they recommend employing a cross-lagged design. In our analysis, we follow this approach and, consistent with Ohrnberger *et al.* (2017) and Kesavayuth *et al.* (2022a), subjective well-being is measured at baseline, lifestyle choices and social capital are measured somewhat later, and physical health is measured at a further time-point. This leads to the following specification:

$$\begin{aligned} PH_{it} = \alpha_0 + \alpha_1 PH_{i,t=0} + \alpha_2 W_{i,t=0} + \alpha_3 L_{i,t-1} \\ + \alpha_4 SC_{i,t-1} + \alpha_5 X_{it} + u_i + \varepsilon_{it}, \end{aligned} \tag{9.43}$$

Table 9.1 Descriptive statistics.

Variable	Description	Mean	Std Dev.
Physical health	0–10 scale; with 0 = worst physical health and 10 = best physical health	7.65	2.11
Baseline physical health	Physical health at baseline	8.03	1.86
Baseline life satisfaction	0–10 scale; with 0 = totally dissatisfied with life and 10 = totally satisfied with life	8.06	1.48
Lagged frequency of physical activity	0–5 scale; with 0 = not at all and 5 = every day	2.59	1.52
Lagged frequency of social interaction	0-6 scale; with 0 = less often than once every 3 months and 6 = every day	3.48	1.46
Lagged frequency of smoking	0–3 scale; with 0 = non-smoker and 3 = smoke daily	0.44	1.03
Lagged volunteer/charity work	Number of hours per week spent in volunteer or charity work	1.03	3.05
Lagged active club member	1 if active member of sporting, hobby, or community-based club or association, 0 otherwise	0.38	0.49
Age	Age of the respondent	44.84	17.43
Household size	Number of persons living in the household	2.88	1.42
Real household income	Real household income in thousands of AUD (base year, 2012)	93.31	66.92
Male	1 if male, 0 if female	0.46	
Married	1 if legally married, 0 otherwise	0.51	
Higher education	1 if graduated at least from college, 0 otherwise	0.61	
Employed	1 if employed, 0 otherwise	0.66	
Unemployed	1 if unemployed, 0 otherwise	0.04	
Not in the labor force	1 if not in the labor force, 0 otherwise	0.31	

Note: Number of observations 75,043.

where PH_{it} is the physical health of individual i at time t; $PH_{i,t=0}$ represents physical health at baseline; $W_{i,t=0}$ is well-being at baseline; $L_{i,t-1}$ is a vector of lifestyle choices (i.e., physical activity, smoking, volunteer/charity work, and being an active member of a social club) at $t-1$; $SC_{i,t-1}$ is a vector representing investments in social capital (i.e., social interaction) at $t-1$; X_{it} is a vector of time-varying variables; u_i is the person-specific error; and ε_{it} is the idiosyncratic error.

The baseline level of well-being is the earliest recorded information for each respondent and, as such, may reflect parental investments in early life and genetic influences. By design, this stock of well-being is orthogonal to the time-varying predictor variables included in the model. Moreover, the use of lagged values for lifestyle choices and social capital captures the fact that investments in health cannot be realized immediately but may take time to materialize.

We hypothesize that individuals' well-being influences their physical health not only directly but also indirectly, through lifestyle choices and social interaction. To estimate the indirect effects, Equation (9.43) can be rewritten with slightly different notation

$$\begin{aligned} PH_{it} = \alpha_0 + \alpha_1 PH_{i,t=0} + \alpha_2 W_{i,t=0} + \alpha_3 PhysAct_{i,t-1}(W_{i,t=0}) \\ + \alpha_4 Smoke_{i,t-1}(W_{i,t=0}) + \alpha_5 Volunteer_{i,t-1}(W_{i,t=0}) \\ + \alpha_6 Club_{i,t-1}(W_{i,t=0}) + \alpha_7 SC_{i,t-1}(W_{i,t=0}) \\ + \alpha_8 X_{it} + u_i + \varepsilon_{it}. \end{aligned} \tag{9.44}$$

To disentangle the direct effect of well-being on physical health from the indirect effects, we proceed by totally differentiating (9.44) with respect to $W_{i,t=0}$. It follows that

$$\frac{dPH}{dW} = \alpha_2 + \left(\frac{\partial PH}{\partial PhysAct} \times \frac{dPhysAct}{dW}\right) + \left(\frac{\partial PH}{\partial Smoke} \times \frac{dSmoke}{dW}\right) + \left(\frac{\partial PH}{\partial Volunteer} \times \frac{dVolunteer}{dW}\right) + \left(\frac{\partial PH}{\partial Club} \times \frac{dClub}{dW}\right) + \left(\frac{\partial PH}{\partial SC} \times \frac{dSC}{dW}\right). \tag{9.45}$$

The first term on the right-hand side of the resulting equation, α_2, represents the *direct effect* of baseline levels of well-being on present physical health. The remaining five terms in parentheses represent the *indirect, mediating effects* of well-being: the first term is the mediating effect through physical activity, the second term is the mediating effect through smoking behavior, and so on, with the last term representing the mediating effect through social capital (for simplicity, subscripts have been omitted).

The mediating effects can be identified using five additional equations

$$\begin{aligned}
\text{PhysAct}_{i,t-1} &= \beta_0 + \beta_1 W_{i,t=0} + \beta_2 X_{i,t-1} + \sigma_i + \upsilon_{i,t-1} \\
\text{Smoke}_{i,t-1} &= \gamma_0 + \gamma_1 W_{i,t=0} + \gamma_2 X_{i,t-1} + \lambda_i + \mu_{i,t-1} \\
\text{Volunteer}_{i,t-1} &= \delta_0 + \delta_1 W_{i,t=0} + \delta_2 X_{i,t-1} + \zeta_i + \psi_{i,t-1} \\
\text{Club}_{i,t-1} &= \eta_0 + \eta_1 W_{i,t=0} + \eta_2 X_{i,t-1} + \varrho_i + \phi_{i,t-1} \\
\text{SC}_{i,t-1} &= \theta_0 + \theta_1 W_{i,t=0} + \theta_2 X_{i,t-1} + \xi_i + \tau_{i,t-1}.
\end{aligned} \tag{9.46}$$

The mediating effects can then be computed as the product of two coefficients. For example, the mediating effect through physical activity is obtained by multiplying the coefficients β_1 in (9.46) and α_3 in (9.44). This approach follows the product-of-coefficients method (Baron and Kenny, 1986; MacKinnon *et al.*, 2007). Our estimations are carried out using linear random effects models with robust standard errors (Cameron and Miller, 2015). The use of random effects is permissible here, given that our key explanatory variable on well-being is observed only at baseline. Our empirical approach is also consistent with past longitudinal mediation analyses (see e.g., Dour *et al.*, 2014; Ohrnberger *et al.*, 2017; Kesavayuth *et al.*, 2021).

9.2.3 *Results*

We begin by examining whether life satisfaction at baseline is associated with the mediators at $t - 1$. Table 9.2 displays the results. Looking across the columns, we see that the estimated coefficient on life satisfaction is statistically significant for lifestyle choices and social capital. This suggests that higher life satisfaction increases the frequency of physical activity and social interaction. It also leads to more time spent on volunteer work and a higher likelihood of being an active member of a social club, while reducing smoking frequency. The beneficial effects of life satisfaction are consistent with a growing body of literature indicating that higher well-being is linked to better economic and behavioral outcomes (e.g., Boehm *et al.*, 2012; Mishra and Smyth, 2014; Kesavayuth and Zikos, 2018, 2024; O'Connor, 2020; Yang and Zikos, 2023, 2024).

Next, we examine whether the mediators at $t - 1$ relate to physical health at t, controlling for life satisfaction at baseline. Table 9.3 presents the results. We find that the mediators are significant in the physical health regression equation. Physical activity and social interaction are associated with better physical health, while smoking has the opposite impact. Additionally, participation in volunteer work and being an active member of a social club tend to increase physical health. However, the estimated coefficient on volunteer work is only marginally significant at the 10% level.

Table 9.2 Random effects regression models for the mediators.

	Physical activity ($t-1$)	**Social interaction ($t-1$)**	**Smoking ($t-1$)**	**Volunteer work ($t-1$)**	**Club member ($t-1$)**
	(1)	(2)	(3)	(4)	(5)
Life satisfaction baseline	0.0545***	0.118***	−0.0549***	0.0510***	0.0257***
	(0.00658)	(0.00661)	(0.00580)	(0.0128)	(0.00197)
Physical health baseline	0.128***	0.0503***	−0.0558***	0.0273**	0.0120***
	(0.00548)	(0.00533)	(0.00457)	(0.0115)	(0.00170)
Age ($t-1$)	−0.00375***	−0.0131***	−0.00349***	0.0251***	0.00174***
	(0.000624)	(0.000582)	(0.000421)	(0.00134)	(0.000204)
Male ($t-1$)	0.300***	−0.122***	0.137***	−0.0701*	0.0594***
	(0.0184)	(0.0175)	(0.0148)	(0.0369)	(0.00601)
Household size ($t-1$)	−0.0433***	−0.106***	−0.00983**	0.0260**	−0.00375**
	(0.00588)	(0.00594)	(0.00391)	(0.0107)	(0.00191)
Real household income ($t-1$)	0.000710***	0.000618***	−0.000294***	−0.000649***	0.000281***
	(0.000110)	(0.000100)	(0.0000504)	(0.000226)	(0.0000374)
Married ($t-1$)	−0.171***	−0.182***	−0.139***	0.0335	−0.0140**
	(0.0190)	(0.0173)	(0.0124)	(0.0364)	(0.00591)
Higher education ($t-1$)	−0.00956	−0.0566***	−0.0202	0.169***	0.0109*
	(0.0179)	(0.0169)	(0.0132)	(0.0350)	(0.00596)
Unemployed ($t-1$)	−0.0525*	0.101***	0.0122	0.564***	0.00395
	(0.0270)	(0.0273)	(0.0147)	(0.0659)	(0.00807)
Not in the labor force ($t-1$)	−0.00936	0.191***	−0.0314***	0.375***	0.0327***
	(0.0167)	(0.0157)	(0.00823)	(0.0371)	(0.00516)
Observations	75,043	75,043	75,043	75,043	75,043

Note: $^{*}p < 0.1$, $^{**}p < 0.05$, $^{***}p < 0.01$. Robust standard errors are in parentheses. The models include a set of dummy variables for the survey waves and for the Australian regions of residence as control variables.

Table 9.3 Random effects regression model for physical health.

	Coefficient	Standard error
Life satisfaction baseline	0.0596***	(0.00820)
Physical health baseline	0.513***	(0.00745)
Age	−0.0237***	(0.000728)
Male	0.0467**	(0.0210)
Household size	0.00256	(0.00619)
Real household income	0.000876***	(0.000108)
Married	0.0483**	(0.0204)
Higher education	0.113***	(0.0199)
Unemployed	−0.103***	(0.0301)
Not in the labor force	−0.424***	(0.0203)
Physical activity $(t-1)$	0.0769***	(0.00454)
Social interaction $(t-1)$	0.0266***	(0.00460)
Smoking $(t-1)$	−0.0741***	(0.00848)
Volunteer work $(t-1)$	0.00377*	(0.00217)
Club member $(t-1)$	0.0285**	(0.0128)
Observations	75,043	

Note: $^{*}p < 0.1$, $^{**}p < 0.05$, $^{***}p < 0.01$. Robust standard errors are in parentheses. The models include a set of dummy variables for the survey waves and for the Australian regions of residence as control variables.

As expected, life satisfaction remains significant and has a positive effect on physical health.

The findings reported thus far suggest that life satisfaction influences physical health not only directly but also indirectly through behavioral pathways. We can formally test this hypothesis by conducting a mediation analysis. Table 9.4 summarizes the results of our mediation analysis for the full sample, while Table 9.5 reports analogous results by gender. Sobel mediation tests are used to assess whether each mediating effect is significantly different from zero (Sobel, 1982; Krull and MacKinnon, 2001).

We find that life satisfaction has significant direct and indirect impacts on physical health. As shown in Table 9.4, the direct effect is positive in the full sample, indicating that individuals with higher life satisfaction tend to have better physical health. The indirect effect is mediated by physical activity, social interaction, smoking,

Table 9.4 Mediation effects on physical health.

	Coefficient	Standard error
(A) Indirect physical activity	0.0042***	(0.0006)
Sobel mediation test	7.4407***	
(B) Indirect social interaction	0.0031***	(0.0006)
Sobel mediation test	5.5012***	
(C) Indirect smoking	0.0041***	(0.0006)
Sobel mediation test	6.4206***	
(D) Indirect volunteer work	0.0002	(0.0001)
Sobel mediation test	1.5925	
(E) Indirect club member	0.0007**	(0.0003)
Sobel mediation test	2.1948**	
(A + B + C + D + E) Total indirect effect	0.0123***	(0.0008)
Sobel mediation test	14.6117***	
(F) Direct effect	0.0596***	(0.0082)
(A) + (B) + (C) + (D) + (E) + (F) Total effect	0.0719***	(0.0082)
Total indirect/Total effect	17.11%	
Observations	75,043	

Note: $^{*}p < 0.1$, $^{**}p < 0.05$, $^{***}p < 0.01$. Significance of the indirect effect can be tested using the Sobel test (Sobel, 1982; Krull and MacKinnon, 2001). This test has been developed for mediation analysis and allows to examine whether the effect of baseline levels of life satisfaction on subsequent physical health operates through each of the possible mediators.

and being an active member of a social club.[10] These indirect effects stem from the positive association between life satisfaction and lifestyle choices, as well as social capital: those who are more satisfied with their life tend to invest more in these areas, which, in turn, benefits their physical health. The estimates show that the total indirect effect accounts for about 17% of the overall link between life satisfaction and physical health. Physical activity represents the largest share (34%) of the total indirect effect, while social interaction, smoking, and active club membership account for 25%, 33%, and 5.7%, respectively.

10 A variance inflation factor (VIF) analysis revealed no evidence of multicollinearity among the mediating variables included in the model.

Table 9.5 Mediation effects on physical health by gender.

	Males		Females	
	Coefficient	Standard error	Coefficient	Standard error
(A) Indirect physical activity	0.0057***	(0.0009)	0.003***	(0.0007)
Sobel mediation test	6.301***		4.1571***	
(B) Indirect social interaction	0.0019**	(0.0008)	0.0041***	(0.0008)
Sobel mediation test	2.2637**		5.2262***	
(C) Indirect smoking	0.0045***	(0.001)	0.0038***	(0.0009)
Sobel mediation test	4.7143***		4.4454***	
(D) Indirect volunteer work	0.0001	(0.0001)	0.0003	(0.0002)
Sobel mediation test	0.8538		1.428	
(E) Indirect club member	0.0012**	(0.0005)	0.0004	(0.0004)
Sobel mediation test	2.3976**		0.945	
(A + B + C + D + E) Total indirect effect	0.0134***	(0.0013)	0.0116***	(0.0011)
Sobel mediation tests	10.5173***		10.5682***	
(F) Direct effect	0.0453***	(0.0117)	0.0715***	(0.0114)
(A) + (B) + (C) + (D) + (E) + (F) Total effect	0.0587***	(0.0118)	0.0831***	(0.0115)
Total indirect/Total effect	22.83%		13.96%	
Observations	34,727		40,316	

Note: See Table 9.4.

Turning to the results by gender in Table 9.5, some interesting patterns emerge. We observe that being an active member of a social club is significant only for males, while physical activity, social interaction, and smoking are significant for both genders. In the disaggregated results, we also note that the share of the indirect effect in the total effect is about 14% for females, but much larger — at 23% — for males. Although we cannot be certain about the reason for this difference, one possible explanation may relate to gender differences in activity participation, which could stem from differences in preferences or motivating factors (e.g., van Uffelen *et al.*, 2017). In this respect, the mediating role of social interaction appears to be more pronounced among females, while physical activity and smoking seem to play a more important role for males.

To address the concern that our results may be influenced by attrition bias — where individuals with lower levels of well-being are more likely to drop out of the panel survey over time — we augmented our specification by including a dummy variable that equals 1 if the respondent leaves the survey in the next wave. The estimates, presented in Table 9.6, are consistent with those in Table 9.4. Physical activity, social interaction, smoking, and being an active member of a social club continue to mediate the link between life satisfaction and physical health. The share of the indirect effect in the total effect remains about 17%.

The results are also robust to the timing of the mediators: we reach qualitatively similar conclusions when using the second-period lagged values of lifestyle choices and social capital. As shown in Table 9.7, using the second-period lags of the mediating variables reinforces our main conclusions by generating even stronger indirect effects. This supports the idea that health investments need time to come into fruition, consistent with our empirical model.

Lastly, we constructed a physical health index by calculating the predicted factor scores from factor analysis. This approach assigns a weight to each item in the index, thereby relaxing the assumption of equal weights. As shown in Table 9.8, the mediating effects of physical activity, social interaction, smoking, and being an active member of a social club remain significant, while the share of the indirect effect in the total effect continues to be approximately 17%, thus lending further support to our main conclusions.

Table 9.6 Mediation effects on physical health, including a dummy variable that takes the value one if the respondent leaves the survey in the following wave.

	Coefficient	Standard error
(A) Indirect physical activity	0.0042***	(0.0006)
Sobel mediation test	7.4353***	
(B) Indirect social interaction	0.0031***	(0.0006)
Sobel mediation test	5.4825***	
(C) Indirect smoking	0.004***	(0.0006)
Sobel mediation test	6.3558***	
(D) Indirect volunteer work	0.0002	(0.0001)
Sobel mediation test	1.5121	
(E) Indirect club member	0.0007**	(0.0003)
Sobel mediation test	2.1276**	
(A + B + C + D + E) Total indirect effect	0.0122***	(0.0009)
Sobel mediation test	14.463***	
(F) Direct effect	0.0605***	(0.0082)
(A) + (B) + (C) + (D) + (E) + (F) Total effect	0.0727***	(0.0083)
Total indirect/Total effect	16.78%	
Observations	75,043	

Note: See Table 9.4.

Table 9.7 Mediation effects on physical health using the second-period lagged values of the mediators.

	Coefficient	Standard error
(A) Indirect physical activity	0.0042***	(0.0006)
Sobel mediation test	6.5521***	
(B) Indirect social interaction	0.0036***	(0.0007)
Sobel mediation test	5.1265***	
(C) Indirect smoking	0.0045***	(0.0008)
Sobel mediation test	5.8122***	
(D) Indirect volunteer work	0.0001	(0.0001)
Sobel mediation test	0.5155	
(E) Indirect club member	0.0011***	(0.0004)
Sobel mediation test	2.8479***	
(A + B + C + D + E) Total indirect effect	0.0135***	(0.001)
Sobel mediation test	13.6116***	
(F) Direct effect	0.0651***	(0.0094)
(A) + (B) + (C) + (D) + (E) + (F) Total effect	0.0786***	(0.0095)
Total indirect/Total effect	17.18%	
Observations	54,450	

Note: See Table 9.4.

Table 9.8 Mediation effects on physical health using an alternative physical health index from factor analysis.

	Coefficient	Standard error
(A) Indirect physical activity	0.0017***	(0.0002)
Sobel mediation test	7.4047***	
(B) Indirect social interaction	0.0013***	(0.0002)
Sobel mediation test	5.4226***	
(C) Indirect smoking	0.0017***	(0.0003)
Sobel mediation test	6.4244***	
(D) Indirect volunteer work	0.0001	(0.0001)
Sobel mediation test	1.5734	
(E) Indirect club member	0.0003**	(0.0001)
Sobel mediation test	2.3785**	
(A + B + C + D + E) Total indirect effect	0.005***	(0.0003)
Sobel mediation test	14.7486***	
(F) Direct effect	0.0243***	(0.0034)
(A) + (B) + (C) + (D) + (E) + (F) Total effect	0.0293***	(0.0034)
Total indirect/Total effect	17.07%	
Observations	75,043	

Note: See Table 9.4.

9.2.4 *Discussion*

Growing evidence suggests that high levels of well-being play a protective role in physical health, yet the underlying pathways remain poorly understood. In this study, we set out to address this gap in the literature by developing a mediation framework to test whether two forms of human capital investments — lifestyle choices and social capital — serve as pathways through which life satisfaction influences subsequent physical health.

Consistent with previous findings in the literature (e.g., Blanchflower and Oswald, 2008; Steptoe *et al.*, 2015), we show that life satisfaction has a significant direct impact on physical health. The direct effect is positive, indicating that individuals with higher life satisfaction tend to have better physical health. Our analysis further reveals that the indirect effect of life satisfaction is mediated by physical activity, social interaction, smoking behavior, and active participation in a social club. The indirect effect accounts for approximately 17% of the overall relationship between life satisfaction and physical health. Physical activity, smoking behavior, and social interaction contribute the largest shares (34%, 33%, and 25%, respectively) to the total indirect effect.

We contribute to the literature by providing new evidence on the behavioral pathways that may help explain the protective role of subjective well-being in physical health. We offer additional evidence that being an active member of a social club is a mediator only for males, while physical activity, social interaction, and smoking are mediators for both males and females. In the disaggregated results by gender, we also find that the share of the indirect effect in the total effect is 14% for females but much larger — at 23% — for males.

What are the implications for public policy? Our findings suggest that certain groups of individuals may be particularly at risk: those (i) with low levels of well-being, (ii) who are not physically active, (iii) who are heavy smokers, or (iv) who are socially isolated. Policies and intervention programs should therefore focus on supporting individuals with these characteristics.

The mediating role of social interaction appears to be more pronounced among females, whereas physical activity and smoking play a more important role among males. This supports the need for gender-specific initiatives to encourage participation. More generally, exploring other potential mediators, such as socioeconomic status and dietary choices, offers a promising direction for future research.

It is worth noting that the methodology employed here is sufficiently general and has been applied in other papers, including one that I co-authored with Dusanee Kesavayuth, Dai Binh Tran, and Joanna Poyago-Theotoky (see also Tran and Zikos, 2019;

Kesavayuth *et al.*, 2021, 2022a). In that paper, we analyze the role of locus of control in shaping health outcomes and healthcare use.[11] Locus of control is a psychological concept that captures "whether or not the person perceives a causal relationship between his own behavior and the reward" (Rotter, 1966, p. 1). We estimate its direct effects and examine whether these effects are mediated by lifestyle choices and social capital. The mathematical foundations of our empirical model mirror those discussed earlier: total derivatives are used to account for all possible channels through which the effects of an independent variable (here, locus of control) are transmitted to the dependent variables (health outcomes and healthcare use).

Further Reading

Ahmed, R., Kesavayuth, D., & Zikos, V. (2018). Does being smarter make you happier? Evidence from Europe. *Journal of Behavioral and Experimental Economics*, 76, 55–67.

Awaworyi Churchill, S. & Smyth, R. (2021). Locus of control and energy poverty. *Energy Economics*, 104, 105648.

Barak, Y. (2006). The immune system and happiness. *Autoimmunity Reviews*, 5, 523–527.

Baron, R. M. & Kenny, D. A. (1986). The moderator–mediator variable distinction in social psychological research: Conceptual, strategic, and statistical considerations. *Journal of Personality and Social Psychology*, 51(6), 1173–1182.

Becker, B. (2015). Public R&D policies and private R&D investment: A survey of the empirical evidence. *Journal of Economic Surveys*, 29(5), 917–942.

Blanchflower, D. G. & Oswald, A. J. (2008). Hypertension and happiness across nations. *Journal of Health Economics*, 27(2), 218–233.

Boehm, J. K., Vie, L. L., & Kubzansky, L. D. (2012). The promise of well-being interventions for improving health risk behaviors. *Current Cardiovascular Risk Reports*, 6, 511–519.

Cameron, C. & Miller, D. (2015). A practitioner's guide to cluster robust inference. *Journal of Human Resources*, 50(2), 317–372.

[11] For more details, the reader is directed to Kesavayuth *et al.* (2020).

Cassiman, B. & Veugelers, R. (2002). R&D cooperation and spillovers: Some empirical evidence from Belgium. *American Economic Review*, 92(4), 1169–1184.

d'Aspremont, C. & Jacquemin, A. (1988). Cooperative and noncooperative R&D in duopoly with spillovers. *American Economic Review*, 78(5), 1133–1137.

Diener, E., Pressman, S. D., Hunter, J., & Delgadillo-Chase, D. (2017). If, why, and when subjective well-being influences health, and future needed research. *Applied Psychology: Health and Well-Being*, 9(2), 133–167.

Dour, H. J., Wiley, J. F., Roy-Byrne, P., Stein, M. B., Sullivan, G., Sherbourne, C. D., Bystritsky, A., Rose, R. D., & Craske, M. G. (2014). Perceived social support mediates anxiety and depressive symptom changes following primary care intervention. *Depression and Anxiety*, 31(5), 436–442.

Eckel, C. & Neary, J. P. (2010). Multi-product firms and flexible manufacturing in the global economy. *The Review of Economic Studies*, 77(1), 188–217.

Ferrett, B. & Zikos, V. (2013). Wage-setting institutions and R&D collaboration networks. *Australian Economic Papers*, 52(2), 61–78.

Gil-Moltó, M. J., Poyago-Theotoky, J., & Zikos, V. (2011). R&D subsidies, spillovers, and privatization in mixed markets. *Southern Economic Journal*, 78(1), 233–255.

Gil-Moltó, M. J., Poyago-Theotoky, J., Rodrigues-Neto, J. A., & Zikos, V. (2020). Mixed oligopoly, cost-reducing research and development, and privatisation. *European Journal of Operational Research*, 283(3), 1094–1106.

Kamien, M. I., Muller, E., & Zang, I. (1992). Research joint ventures and R&D cartels. *The American Economic Review*, 1293–1306.

Kesavayuth, D., Lee, S. H., & Zikos, V. (2018). Merger and innovation incentives in a differentiated industry. *International Journal of the Economics of Business*, 25(2), 207–221.

Kesavayuth, D., Liang, Y., & Zikos, V. (2018). An active lifestyle and cognitive function: Evidence from China. *The Journal of the Economics of Ageing*, 12, 183–191.

Kesavayuth, D., Manasakis, C., & Zikos, V. (2016). Endogenous R&D networks among upstream firms. *Managerial and Decision Economics*, 37(2), 79–94.

Kesavayuth, D., Poyago-Theotoky, J., Tran, D. B., & Zikos, V. (2020). Locus of control, health and healthcare utilization. *Economic Modelling*, 86, 227–238.

Kesavayuth, D., Rosenman, R. E., & Zikos, V. (2015). Personality and health satisfaction. *Journal of Behavioral and Experimental Economics*, 54, 64–73.

Kesavayuth, D., Rosenman, R. E., & Zikos, V. (2016). Retirement, personality, and well-being. *Economic Inquiry*, 54(2), 733–750.

Kesavayuth, D., Rosenman, R. E., & Zikos, V. (2018). Retirement and health behaviour. *Applied Economics*, 50(54), 5859–5876.

Kesavayuth, D., Rosenman, R. E., & Zikos, V. (2020). The dynamic effects of retirement on well-being. *Applied Economics*, 52(54), 5921–5935.

Kesavayuth, D., Rosenman, R. E., & Zikos, V. (2022). Leaving the labor market: Exit routes, personality traits and well-being. *Plos One*, 17(3), e0263670.

Kesavayuth, D., Shangkhum, P., & Zikos, V. (2021). Subjective well-being and healthcare utilization: A mediation analysis. *SSM–Population Health*, 14, 100796.

Kesavayuth, D., Shangkhum, P., & Zikos, V. (2022a). Well-being and physical health: A mediation analysis. *Journal of Happiness Studies*, 1–31.

Kesavayuth, D., Shangkhum, P., & Zikos, V. (2022b). Building physical health: What is the role of mental health? *Bulletin of Economic Research*, 74(2), 457–483.

Kesavayuth, D. & Zikos, V. (2009). Endogenous contracts in unionized oligopoly. *Labour*, 23(2), 209–235.

Kesavayuth, D. & Zikos, V. (2012). Upstream and downstream horizontal R&D networks. *Economic Modelling*, 29(3), 742–750.

Kesavayuth, D. & Zikos, V. (2013). R&D versus output subsidies in mixed markets. *Economics Letters*, 118(2), 293–296.

Kesavayuth, D. & Zikos, V. (2013). International and national R&D networks in unionized oligopoly. *Labour*, 27(1), 18–37.

Kesavayuth, D. & Zikos, V. (2016). Price or quantity? A new irrelevance result for mixed markets. *Australian Economic Papers*, 55(1), 29–42.

Kesavayuth, D. & Zikos, V. (2018). Happy people are less likely to be unemployed: Psychological evidence from panel data. *Contemporary Economic Policy*, 36(2), 277–291.

Kesavayuth, D. & Zikos, V. (2024). Mental health and obesity. *Applied Economic Analysis*, 32(94), 41–61.

Kesavayuth, D. & Zikos, V. (2025). Mental health and financial risk attitudes: Panel data evidence from Australia. *Contemporary Economic Policy*, 43(2), 178–198.

Krull, J. L. & MacKinnon, D. P. (2001). Multilevel modeling of individual and group level mediated effects. *Multivariate Behavioral Research*, 36(2), 249–277.

López, Á. L. & Vives, X. (2019). Overlapping ownership, R&D spillovers, and antitrust policy. *Journal of Political Economy*, 127(5), 2394–2437.

MacKinnon, D. P., Fairchild, A. J., & Fritz, M. S. (2007). Mediation analysis. *Annual Review of Psychology*, 58, 593–614.

Magnani, E. & Zhu, R. (2018). Does kindness lead to happiness? Voluntary activities and subjective well-being. *Journal of Behavioral and Experimental Economics*, 77, 20–28.

Manasakis, C., Petrakis, E., & Zikos, V. (2014). Downstream Research Joint Venture with upstream market power. *Southern Economic Journal*, 80(3), 782–802.

Manasakis, C. & Zikos, V. (2007). Unions' and firms' attitudes towards research joint ventures: When will the incentives be aligned? *Labour*, 21(1), 135–156.

Mishra, V. & Smyth, R. (2014). It pays to be happy (if you are a man): Subjective wellbeing and the gender wage gap in urban China. *International Journal of Manpower*, 35(3), 392–414.

O'Connor, K. J. (2020). Life satisfaction and noncognitive skills: Effects on the likelihood of unemployment. *Kyklos*, 73(4), 568–604.

O'Connor, K. J. & Graham, C. (2019). Longer, more optimistic, lives: Historic optimism and life expectancy in the United States. *Journal of Economic Behavior & Organization*, 168, 374–392.

Ohrnberger, J., Fichera, E., & Sutton, M. (2017). The relationship between physical and mental health: A mediation analysis. *Social Science & Medicine*, 195, 42–49.

Pavot, W. & Diener, E. (1993). Review of the satisfaction with life scale. *Psychological Assessment*, 5(2), 164–172.

Powdthavee, N. (2010). *The Happiness Equation: The Surprising Economics of Our Most Valuable Asset.* London, Icon Books Ltd.

Powdthavee, N. (2015). Would you like to know what makes people happy? An overview of the datasets on subjective well-being. *Australian Economic Review*, 48(3), 314–320.

Poyago-Theotoky, J. (2024). *Mixed Oligopoly and Public Enterprises.* Cambridge, Cambridge University Press.

Radić, M., Ravasi, D., & Munir, K. (2021). Privatization: Implications of a shift from state to private ownership. *Journal of Management*, 47(6), 1596–1629.

Rasciute, S. & Downward, P. (2010). Health or happiness? What is the impact of physical activity on the individual? *Kyklos*, 63(2), 256–270.

Rickman, N. & Zikos, V. (2016). Endogenous R&D networks when labour unions have preferences over wages and employment. *Economics of Innovation and New Technology*, 25(1), 1–13.

Rotter, J. B. (1966). Generalized expectancies for internal versus external control of reinforcement. *Psychological Monographs*, 80(1), 1–28.

Rowan, P. J., Haas, D., Campbell, J. A., Maclean, D. R., & Davidson, K. W. (2005). Depressive symptoms have an independent, gradient risk for coronary heart disease incidence in a random, population-based sample. *Annals of Epidemiology*, 15(4), 316–320.

Ryff, C. D., Radler, B. T., & Friedman, E. M. (2015). Persistent psychological well-being predicts improved self-rated health over 9–10 years: Longitudinal evidence from MIDUS. *Health Psychology Open*, 2(2), 1–11.

Shangkhum, P. & Zikos, V. (2023). New evidence on the relationship between mental and physical health. *Economics Letters*, 233, 111378.

Sobel, M. E. (1982). Asymptotic confidence intervals for indirect effects in structural equation models. *Sociological Methodology*, 13, 290–312.

Sovinsky, M. (2022). Do research joint ventures serve a collusive function? *Journal of the European Economic Association*, 20(1), 430–475.

Steptoe, A., Deaton, A., & Stone, A. A. (2015). Subjective well-being, health, and ageing. *The Lancet*, 385(9968), 640–648.

Stiglitz, J. E., Sen, A., & Fitoussi, J.P. (2010). Report by the commission on the measurement of economic performance and social progress, *Paris: Commission on the Measurement of Economic Performance and Social Progress.*

Surtees, P. G., Wainwright, N. W. J., Luben, R. N., Wareham, N. J., Bingham, S. A., & Khaw, K. T. (2008). Psychological distress, major depressive disorder, and risk of stroke. *Neurology*, 70(10), 788–794.

Tran, D. B., Pham, T. D. N., & Nguyen, T. T. (2021). The influence of education on women's well-being: Evidence from Australia. *Plos One*, 16(3), e0247765.

Tran, T. T. & Zikos, V. (2018). Endogenous free trade agreements and international R&D networks. *The Manchester School*, 86(5), 641–664.

Tran, T. T. & Zikos, V. (2017). R&D networks among suppliers and manufacturers. *Economic Modelling*, 60, 151–161.

Tran, B. D. & Zikos, V. (2019). The causal effect of retirement on health: Understanding the mechanisms. *Australian Economic Review*, 52(4), 427–446.

Vanderweele, T. J. (2015). *Explanation in Causal Inference: Methods for Mediation and Interaction*. New York, Oxford University Press.

VanderWeele, T. J., & Tchetgen Tchetgen, E. J. (2017). Mediation analysis with time varying exposures and mediators. *Journal of the Royal Statistical Society. Series B, Statistical Methodology*, 79(3), 917–938.

van Uffelen, J. G., Khan, A., & Burton, N. W. (2017). Gender differences in physical activity motivators and context preferences: A population-based study in people in their sixties. *BMC Public Health*, 17(1), 1–11.

Windle, G., Hughes, D., Linck, P., Russell, I., & Woods, B. (2010). Is exercise effective in promoting mental well-being in older age? A systematic review. *Aging & Mental Health*, 14(6), 652–69.

Yang, L. & Zikos, V. (2022). Healthy mind in healthy body: Identifying the causal effect of mental health on physical health. *Economics Letters*, 213, 110358.

Yang, L. & Zikos, V. (2023). Mental health and smoking behavior. *Economic Modelling*, 126, 106407.

Yang, L. & Zikos, V. (2024). Mind over matter: The impact of mental health on energy poverty. *Energy Research & Social Science*, 117, 103703.

Yang, L. & Zikos, V. (2025). Mental and physical health: The mediating role of physical activity. *Applied Economics*, 57(25), 3473–3488.

Zikos, V. (2007a). A reappraisal of the irrelevance result in mixed duopoly: A note on R&D competition. *Economics Bulletin*, 12(8), 1–6.

Zikos, V. (2007b). Stackelberg mixed oligopoly with asymmetric subsidies. *Economics Bulletin*, 12(13), 1–5.

Zikos, V. (2010). R&D collaboration networks in mixed oligopoly. *Southern Economic Journal*, 77(1), 189–212.

Zikos, V. (2025). Do gender differences in mental health contribute to gender differences in physical health? An instrumental variables approach. *Australian Economic Review*, 58(1), 21–32.

Index

A

adjoint, 14
adjugate of a matrix, 14
area under a curve, 117
array
  of real numbers, 3
associative law, 7

B

boundary solution, 91
budget constraint, 69, 81, 93, 96

C

capital, 37, 67–68, 85–86, 176, 179, 181–183, 186, 188, 190, 192
chain rule, 33
Cobb-Douglas production function, 37, 85
cofactor matrix, 13–14, 21–23
commutative law, 6
comparative static analysis, 57, 67, 173
complementary function, 137
complementary slackness, 92
concave function, 45, 50
constant coefficient
  differential equation, 134
constant term
  differential equation, 133–134, 138, 141, 143
constraint qualification, 101
continuity, 174
continuous function, 29, 31, 33, 118, 148
convergence, 142, 157
convergent time path, 142
convex function, 39, 49, 100
convex set, 39–41
cost function, 61, 165

D

data, 178
definite integral
  as area under a curve, 117
  properties of, 120
deletion
  of rows or columns, 13
demand
  excess, 141
  for capital, 68
  for labor, 68
  function, 68
dependent variable
  of differential equation, 134, 139, 145
  of equation, 34
  of regression model, 178, 192
derivative
  concept of, 26
  first, 41, 43, 66
  partial, 29
  second, 41–42, 44–45, 65
  total, 31
determinant
  defined, 12

diagonal
  elements of matrix, 8
differentiability
  continuity in relation to, 27
differentiable function, 28, 31
differential
  rules of, 31
  total, 30
differential calculus, 44
differential equation
  complete equation, 137
  definite solution of, 136, 138
  exact, 148
  first-order linear, 134
  general solution of, 136, 138
  homogeneous, 136
  non-homogeneous, 136
  reduced equation, 137
  verification of the solution of, 139
diminishing returns, 165
distributive law
  of matrix operations, 7
divergence, 123–124
domain, 42, 45–46, 50–51
dynamic analysis, 107, 140
dynamics
  of market price, 140

E

empirical research vs. theoretical, 175
envelope theorem, 66
equality
  between matrices, 4
  constraints, 73
equation system, 11, 21, 68, 70, 75, 79, 97–98, 104, 164, 167, 169, 171, 192
equation(s)
  complete, 137
  differential, 133
  homogeneous, 136
  non-homogeneous, 138, 146
  quadratic, 64, 165
  reduced, 137, 139
equilibrium, 107, 133, 140–143, 156–157, 163, 167–173
equilibrium condition, 107
exact differential equation, 148, 149, 152–153, 155
excess demand, 141–143
exogenous variables, 61, 164
extreme value(s), 44

F

factor
  analysis, 179
  common, 153
  integrating, 153
first derivative, 41
first-order condition, 65–66, 68, 75, 77–78, 80, 85, 90–92, 166
function
  Cobb-Douglas, 37, 85
  complementary, 137
  concave vs. convex, 41
  continuous, 29, 31, 33, 118, 134, 148
  continuously differentiable, 31
  cost, 61, 68, 165
  demand, 141, 164
  differentiable, 27, 28, 33, 65, 90, 100
  domain of, 42, 45–46, 50–51
  graph of, 27, 43
  implicit, 34–35, 37
  inflection point of, 44, 66
  inverse, 68
  Lagrangian, 74–75, 77–79, 81, 83–85, 92–97
  linear, 49, 52, 100–101
  objective, 57, 67, 73–74, 77, 82, 86, 101–102, 166, 170
  profit, 55, 61, 82, 166
  quadratic, 64, 165

quasi-concave vs. quasi-convex, 49
saddle point of, 62
social welfare, 168, 170–171
supply, 140
value, 67

H

Hessian matrix, 39, 47–48, 52–55, 60–62, 69–70, 76–78, 84, 86
homogeneous equation, 137
Hotelling's lemma, 68

I

identity
matrix, 7
implicit function, 35
implicit function theorem, 34, 37
indefinite integral, 110, 117
independent variable, 30, 34, 77, 134, 176, 179, 192
indifference curve, 36–37
inequality constraint, 89, 95, 101
infinite
limit of integration, 122
inflection point, 44, 66
initial condition, 109, 136, 138–140, 145–146, 157–158
input, 37
instantaneous rate of change, 108
integral
applications of, 124
improper, 124
indefinite, 117, 122
of a multiple, 113
of a sum, 112
particular, 137
properties of, 120
integral calculus, 139
integrand, 107, 109–110, 112–114, 123, 127
integrating factor, 151, 153
integration
by parts, 115
concept of, 108
constant of, 109, 150, 154
limits of, 117, 120
integration rules
exponential rule, 112
integration by parts, 115
logarithmic rule, 111
multiplication rule, 113
power rule, 110
substitution rule, 113
sum-difference rule, 112
intercept, 165
interval, 119
inverse function, 164
inverse matrices
definition of, 10
finding, 11
properties of, 12
investment
cost-reducing, 163
health, 176, 181
R&D, 163–167, 170
social capital, 181
Isoquant, 37–38

K

Kuhn-Tucker conditions, 89–98, 100–105
Kuhn-Tucker sufficiency theorem, 101–102

L

lag, 179, 181, 188
Lagrange multiplier, 73–74, 78, 81, 83, 92, 94, 96
equality constraints, 74
interpretation of, 81
Lagrangian function, 74, 103
limit
for differentiability, 26
of integration, 117, 120, 122
linear combination, 41
linear constraint, 101
linear function, 49, 52

local
optimum, 58–66, 77–80, 84, 100
logarithmic-function rule
of integration, 111–112

M

marginal cost, 164–165
marginal product, 37
marginal rate of substitution, 36
marginal utility, 36, 82
market price, dynamics of, 140
matrices
addition of, 4
adjoint, 14
as arrays, 3
cofactor, 13
defined, 3
determinants, 12
Hessian, 47
multiplication of, 5
operations of, 4
singular vs. non-singular, 16
square, 7
subtraction, 4
transpose, 9
maximum, 44
maximum value function, 67
minimum, 44
minor
bordered principal, 47, 53
multiple roots, 64

N

n-variables, 67, 76
N-th derivative test, 65–66
necessary condition, 2, 59, 63–64
necessary-and-sufficient condition, 3
neighborhood, 35, 44, 59, 63–64
non-homogeneous equation, 136–139, 141, 143, 146, 148, 153
non-negative orthant, 99, 101
null matrix, 8

O

objective function, 74, 86, 94, 101–102, 107, 169
optimal value, 75, 82
optimization
unconstrained, 58
ordered pair, 45
orthant, 99
orthogonal matrix, 10

P

parameter, 67, 74, 81, 164
partial derivative, 25, 29, 32, 34–35, 67, 92, 96, 150
particular integral
of first-order differential equation, 137
period, 188
period analysis, 178
power-function rule
in finding total differential, 31
of integration, 110
price, 67–69, 133, 140–143, 156
time path of, 142
primitive function, 108–110, 112, 114, 119
principal minor
bordered Hessian, 47, 53
product
marginal, 37
matrix multiplication, 5
of input, 37, 61, 68
product rule, 31
production function, 37
maximization of, 85
slope of isoquant, 37
profit function, 55, 67–68, 170
profit, maximization of, 61, 68, 82, 166, 169

Q

quadratic, 64
qualitative information, 179
quotient rule, 31

R

rate of change, 41, 109
real number, 3
reduced equation, 137
roots, 64
row of matrix, 12–17, 77

S

saddle point, 62
scalar, 4, 8, 12–13
scalar multiplication, 4
second derivative, 43, 65
second-derivative test, 63
second-order condition
  in relation to concavity and convexity, 47
  in relation to quasi-concavity and quasi-convexity, 52
  necessary vs. sufficient, 59, 76, 100
set(s)
  convex vs.non-convex, 40
slope, 27, 36–38, 41–43, 58, 63–64, 165
social welfare function, 163–164, 166, 168–171, 173
square matrix, 9–10, 12–13, 15–16, 18, 47
statics, 57
strictly concave function, 43, 45–46, 48–49, 52, 54–55, 61, 69
strictly convex function, 43, 46–49, 52
strictly quasi-concave function, 52–53
strictly quasi-convex function, 52–53
substitution
  marginal rate of, 36
sufficiency theorem, Kuhn-Tucker, 101
sufficient condition, 2–3, 18, 60–61, 64, 79, 83–84, 86, 90
sum-difference rule
  integrals, 112
  total differentials, 31
supply, 140, 143, 156
symmetric matrix, 10

T

time path, 108, 133, 142, 156
  convergent, 142
  of price, 140
total differential, 25, 30, 32–33, 36–37, 148–149
total differentiation, 161
transpose of matrix, 1, 9–10

U

utility, 36–37, 54, 69–70, 81, 93, 95–96, 103, 162
utility maximization, 36, 69, 81, 103

V

variable(s)
  choice, 78, 90–92, 94
  dependent vs. independent, 28, 31, 33–34, 178–179
  endogenous vs. exogenous, 61, 164
vector, 181

W

weighted average, 45–46

Z

zero matrix, 8–9

www.ingramcontent.com/pod-product-compliance
Ingram Content Group UK Ltd.
Pitfield, Milton Keynes, MK11 3LW, UK
UKHW021838100926
8556IPUK00004B/418

9 789819 814107